MW01267544

CONTENTS

Author: **Katherine Engle, M.A.**
Managing Editor: Alan Christopherson, M.S.
Revision Editor: Christine E. Wilson, B.A., M.A.
Illustrator: Kyle Bennett
Graphic Designers: Annette Walker
Alpha Omega Graphics

Alpha Omega Publications®

804 N. 2nd Ave. E., Rock Rapids, IA 51246-1759
© MMI by Alpha Omega Publications, Inc. All rights reserved.
LIFEPAC is a registered trademark of Alpha Omega Publications, Inc.

SPANISH II: UNIT ONE
INTRODUCTION

Spanish II Unit One is focused on intensive grammar review in preparation for the second year of foreign language study. Upon completion of this book, you will have a thorough review of grammatical concepts that will appear many times in the coming chapters, such as agreement and verb conjugation. This unit was designed to help you cover enough grammar to comprehend a variety of situations. A good understanding of the grammar in this chapter will enable you to practice future vocabulary with greater ease and retention.

Two present tenses are covered: one simple (the present indicative) and one compound (the present progressive). This is an introduction to the concept of multiple expressions of tense, as we will see again when we study the past tenses.

Unit One reviews the "basics" thoroughly: expressing date, time, and numbers. It's an enjoyable review for most students, who feel they are "good" at counting, etc. Furthermore, it is wise to know these terms well, for can you imagine holding a conversation, in any language, that doesn't include a date, a time, or a number? When

you know these simple topics well, you are less likely to stumble or falter during oral activities in particular. It is a whole segment of knowledge which is stress-free and builds up your self-confidence.

In this unit the reflexive form of verbs in the present tense is discussed. Although the reflexive exists in the English language, its use is not nearly as extensive or as important as it is to the Spanish language. Once the concept is firmly grasped, it will not be a hindrance when you begin to study the past tense. Like the "basics" described above, a thorough review of the reflexive is provided so that it doesn't impede learning later. You will already have acquired that knowledge and will be able to apply it to other expressions of tense.

You will notice that no vocabulary is reviewed in this unit. If vocabulary were included, the unit would become rather unwieldy in scope. The unit attempts to stay within the range of expression for a second-year foreign language student. As stated before, the focus of this unit is grammar and mechanics. It gives you the tools to acquire new concepts and vocabulary.

OBJECTIVES

Read these objectives. These objectives tell what you should be able to do when you have completed this LIFEPAC®.

1. Differentiate and use the simple present and present progressive tenses appropriately.

2. Count as high as you can.

3. Relate the date and time, as well as figure and compare the dates and times of future events.

4. Describe people, places, and things using noun/adjective agreement.

5. Differentiate and use *ser* and *estar*.

6. Use reflexive verb forms to discuss your personal care habits and those of others.

I. REVIEW THE PRESENT TENSE

Before we begin a review of verb forms, we need to discuss the concept of subject and verb agreement in sentences. **Look at the following English sentences.**

Susana reads a magazine.
Tomás travels to South America.

▶ **Answer the following questions.**

1.1   a.   Who is doing the action in the first sentence? _____

      b.   Who is the subject? _____

      c.   What is the action of the first sentence? _____

      d.   What is the verb? _____

      Analyze the second sentence in the same manner.

      e.   The subject is _____

      f.   The verb is _____

A complete English sentence has two elements: a subject (the "who") and an agreeing verb form (the action). It is the same for foreign languages. **Read the following Spanish sentences.**

Manuela habla español.
Jorge vive en México.

▶ **Answer the following questions for the first sentence.**

1.2   a.   The subject is   _____
      b.   The verb is   _____

      Continue with the second sentence.

      c.   The subject is   _____
      d.   The verb is   _____

Since each sentence contains a subject and an agreeing verb form, we know they are complete. As with the English language, subjects may be expressed as proper nouns or pronouns.

1.3   What is the function of a pronoun within a sentence? _____

Review the Spanish subject pronouns:

yo (I)	nosotros (we, masculine) nosotras (we, feminine)
tú (you, informal)	vosotros (all of you, informal, masculine, Spain only) vosotras (all of you, informal, feminine, Spain only)
él (he) ella (she) usted (you, formal)	ellos (they, masculine) ellas (they, feminine) ustedes (all of you)

In this text:
Usted will be abbreviated as *Ud.*
Ustedes will be abbreviated as *Uds.*
Vosotros and *vosotras* are translated as *all of you,* in an informal situation. Their use in the Spanish-speaking world is limited to Spain; therefore, they are only presented for the sake of exposition in this text. They will not be used in the exercises.

Practice the subject pronouns briefly before continuing with verb forms. Decide which pronoun from the chart above would replace these names and other nouns.

1.4   a.   María   _____

b.   María y yo   _____

c.   Tomás   _____

d.   Tomás y María   _____

e.   las señoras   _____

f.   mi amiga   _____

g.   Ud. y Uds.   _____

h.   tú y Consuela   _____

i.   la clase y yo   _____

j.   usted y yo   _____

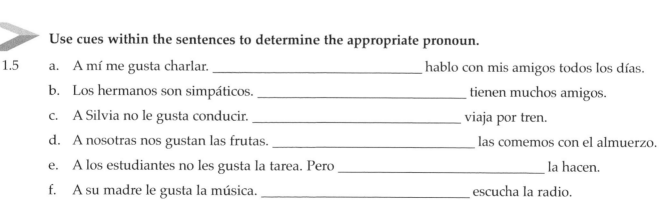

Tomás y María

Use cues within the sentences to determine the appropriate pronoun.

1.5   a.   A mí me gusta charlar. _____ hablo con mis amigos todos los días.

b.   Los hermanos son simpáticos. _____ tienen muchos amigos.

c.   A Silvia no le gusta conducir. _____ viaja por tren.

d.   A nosotras nos gustan las frutas. _____ las comemos con el almuerzo.

e.   A los estudiantes no les gusta la tarea. Pero _____ la hacen.

f.   A su madre le gusta la música. _____ escucha la radio.

g. A Marcos le gusta el fútbol. _____ juega los sábados.

h. A Juan y a ti les gusta correr. _____ hacen jogging por la mañana.

Decide which pronoun would be used in the response to each question.

1.6   a. ¿Quieres tú bailar?   ¿ _____ ? No, gracias.

b. ¿Cocinan Uds. bien?   ¿ _____ ? No muy bien.

c. ¿Escucha ella?   ¿ _____ ? Sí, siempre.

d. ¿Puede Ud. hablar?   ¿ _____ ? Ahora no.

e. ¿Vienen mis amigos?   ¿ _____ ? Todavía no.

f. ¿Trabaja tu padre?   ¿ _____ ? Sí, en una oficina.

g. ¿Entramos nosotros aquí?   ¿ _____ ? No, por aquí.

Now we can discuss regular verb endings for the present tense.

trabajar—to work

yo	**trabajo**	nosotros nosotras	**trabajamos**
tú	**trabajas**	vosotros vosotras	**trabajáis**
él ella Ud.	**trabaja**	ellos ellas Uds.	**trabajan**

Answer the following questions.

1.7   a. What was removed from *trabajar*?   _____

b. How was *trabajar* changed after that?   _____

Fill in the chart below with the correct endings.

1.8

a. yo	d. nosotros nosotras
b. tú	e. vosotros vosotras
c. él ella Ud.	f. ellos ellas Uds.

4

We can conclude, therefore, that there are two steps to conjugating (forming) verbs.

1.9   What was dropped from *trabajar*?

    a. _____

What was added to form *yo trabajo? tú trabajas?*, etc.

    b. _____

There is one more important point to keep in mind: the implied subject.

    c. What is meant by "implied"? _____

Please note how each form has its own special ending. That means that for regular verbs, "–o" can only be paired with *yo.*

    d. In that case, we know that ANY verb ending in "–o" can ONLY be translated in the present indicative as "I...." If *cantar* is *to sing*, how do you translate *canto*? _____

    e. If *ayudar* is *to help*, how do you translate *ayudo*? _____

The implied subject means that writing the subject pronoun all the time is unnecessary, because the individual verb endings signal who is performing the action.

    f. If *bailar* means *to dance*, how do you translate *bailamos*? _____

    g. How do you translate *bailas*? _____

    h. How do you translate *bailo*? _____

Try filling in this chart with the forms of the verb *estudiar* (to study).

1.10 a. Once you drop the *–ar*, what is left? _____

That is the stem of the infinitive.

estudiar—to study

b. yo	e. nosotros nosotras
c. tú	f. vosotros vosotras **estudiáis**
d. él ella Ud.	g. ellos ellas Uds.

Translate each form three different ways.

1.11 a. estudio _____

    b. estudias _____

    c. estudia _____

    d. estudiamos _____

    e. estudian _____

Now that you have thoroughly reviewed subject pronouns and –*ar* verb endings, review the –*er* and –*ir* endings.

–ER verb endings

yo	-o	nosotros nosotras	-emos
tú	-es	vosotros vosotras	-éis
él ella Ud.	-e	ellos ellas Uds.	-en

– IR verb endings

yo	-o	nosotros nosotras	-imos
tú	-es	vosotros vosotras	-ís
él ella Ud.	-e	ellos ellas Uds.	-en

Fill in the charts with the appropriate forms of the verbs given. Remember to remove the infinitive endings before adding on the verb endings. The first box has been done for you.

beber—to drink

1.12

a. yo	**bebo**	d. nosotros nosotras	**bebemos**
b. tú	**bebes**	e. vosotros vosotras	**bebéis**
c. él ella Ud.	**bebe**	f. ellos ellas Uds.	**beben**

1.13   **abrir**—to open

a. yo	d. nosotros nosotras
b. tú	e. vosotros vosotras **abrís**

c. él
    ella
    Ud.
	f. ellos
	    ellas
	    Uds.

Some final words on verb form and expression—in order to express negation ("no," "don't," etc.), place "no" in front of the verb form.

Yo abro.   **Yo no abro.**

(I open)   (I don't open.)

In order to ask a question, either place question marks around the phrase or invert (flip) the verb form and the subject.

Yo abro.   **¿Yo abro?**

(I open)   (Should I <u>open</u> [it]?)

                      ¿Abro yo?

                      (Should <u>I</u> be the one to open [it]?)

Change the italicized verb form in each paragraph to agree with the new subjects. Write each new form on the blank.

1.14   a.   Carlos *bebe* agua mineral pero yo _____ refrescos. Mi hermanita
            _____ leche. Es buena para los jovencitos. Cuando vamos al restaurante,
            _____ Coca-Cola.

       b.   Mi familia *vive* en un apartamento. La familia de mis amigos _____ en una casa
            grande. Pero no me molesta. Me gusta _____ en la ciudad. Visito mucho a mis
            primos que _____ en una granja.

       c.   *Camino* para la salud. Muchas veces mi mamá _____ conmigo y entonces
            nosotros _____ varios kilómetros. Nos gusta _____ juntos.
            A veces mi hermana _____ con nosotros.

Fill in the blanks with the proper forms of the given verbs.

1.15   a.   José _____ mi champú. (usar)

        b.   Uds. se _____ bien. (llevar)

        c.   Yo _____ por la noche. (estudiar)

        d.   Tú y yo nos _____ las cabezas. (golpear)

        e.   Nosotros nos _____ el tobillo. (torcer)

        f.   Ustedes _____ una carta. (escribir)

        g.   La clase _____ de la escuela. (salir)

        h.   Ustedes _____ la pelota. (buscar)

        i.   Mariana me _____ un regalo. (dar)

        j.   Alonso _____ al autobús. (subir)

Choose elements from the columns below in order to translate and write sentences.

A	B	C
yo	beber	las matemáticas
tú	abrir	la leche
nosotros	estudiar	la puerta
las amigas	escribir	la carta
Ud.	aprender	la lección
Uds. y yo	comprender	el agua
la familia	llevar	el libro

Translate these five sentences based on the vocabulary given above.

1.16   a.   You open the book. _____

        b.   You and I learn the lesson. _____

        c.   The family writes the letter. _____

        d.   I understand math. _____

        e.   The friends study the lesson. _____

Now, create five original sentences based on the vocabulary given above.

1.17   a.   _____

        b.   _____

        c.   _____

        d.   _____

        e.   _____

> **Read the following passage.**

Planeamos muchas actividades. *Participamos* en los deportes en la escuela. El sábado, por la noche, *miramos* una película. *Pasamos* una buena noche allí. *Regresamos* a casa para la medianoche. *Subimos* al autobús para ir a la iglesia con la familia el domingo. No *vivimos* lejos de la iglesia. *Comemos* el desayuno después. *Descansamos* por la tarde. *Preparamos* la tarea por la noche.

Change all the italicized verb forms to the *yo* form.

1.18   a. _____   f. _____

         b. _____   g. _____

         c. _____   h. _____

         d. _____   i. _____

         e. _____   j. _____

Now, change those *yo* forms to the *tú* forms.

1.19   a. _____   f. _____

         b. _____   g. _____

         c. _____   h. _____

         d. _____   i. _____

         e. _____   j. _____

> **Comprehension questions—you may answer in English.**

1.20   a. Where are they every Saturday night? _____

         b. How do they travel to church?_____

         c. Where do they play sports?_____

         d. Do they eat breakfast before or after church? _____

         e. At what time do they return home from the film? _____

Adult check _____

                              Initial   Date

Review the material in this section in preparation for the Self Test. This Self Test will check your mastery of this particular section. The items missed on this Self Test will indicate specific areas where restudy is needed for mastery.

SELF TEST 1

1.01   **Match each form to the agreeing subject for each group.** (1 pt. each)

1.	yo	_____	a.	como
2.	nosotros	_____	b.	come
3.	tú	_____	c.	comemos
4.	Ud.	_____	d.	comen
5.	ellos	_____	e.	comes

6.	Uds.	_____	f.	trabaja
7.	tú	_____	g.	trabajas
8.	yo	_____	h.	trabajo
9.	Ud.	_____	i.	trabajamos
10.	nosotras	_____	j.	trabajan

11.	tú	_____	k.	viven
12.	nosotros	_____	l.	vivimos
13.	ella	_____	m.	vives
14.	yo	_____	n.	vive
15.	ellos	_____	o.	vivo

1.02   **Write the correct indicated form of the verb given.** (1 pt. each)

a.   Juan (escoger)   _____

b.   el equipo (ganar)   _____

c.   tú (subir)   _____

d.   nosotros (abrir)   _____

e.   yo (sudar)   _____

f.   mi mamá (vender)   _____

g.   las hermanas (cubrir)   _____

h.   Ud. y yo (salir)   _____

i.   Jorge, Blas y Elena (chiflar) _____

j.   Uds. (hacer)   _____

1.03   **Translate, using the verbs in the box.** (1 pt. each)

hablar	vender	correr
pasar	llevar	subir
cantar	hacer	describir

a.   we sing   _____

b.   I sell   _____

c.   he gets on (bus)   _____

d.   they run   _____

e.   you sing   _____

f.   he carries   _____

g.   all of you pass   _____

h.   I describe   _____

i.   you speak   _____

j.   she does   _____

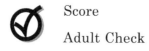
Score   _____

Adult Check   _____

Initial   Date

II. REVIEW STEM-CHANGING VERBS OF THE PRESENT TENSE

Look closely at the forms of the verb *querer* (to want).

querer—to want

yo	**quiero**	nosotros nosotras	**queremos**
tú	**quieres**	vosotros vosotras	**queréis**
él ella Ud.	**quiere**	ellos ellas Uds.	**quieren**

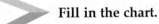 **Complete the following questions.**

2.1   a.   Which forms have a different stem from the infinitive, and how are they different?

_____

b.   Draw a line around the changed forms.

c.   Which forms are left out? _____

_____

Once you have drawn that shape, it should resemble a shoe. For this reason, the verbs we are reviewing are nicknamed "shoe verbs." Although they are considered regular, they all have a pattern of change in all but the *nosotros* and *vosotros* forms. What change occurred in *querer*?

d.   What did the *e* change to? _____

Below is a table to fill in for the verb *pensar*. It follows the same pattern as *querer*.

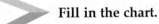 **Fill in the chart.**

2.2   **pensar**—to think about

a. yo		d. nosotros nosotras	
b. tú		e. vosotros vosotras	**pensáis**

c. él
   ella
   Ud
		f. ellos
		   ellas
		   Uds.	

12

Here is a list of "e-ie" verbs that follow the same pattern as *querer*.

confesar	to confess
defender	to defend
despertar	to wake up (someone)
encender	to light, turn on
entender	to understand
fregar	to scrub
helar	to freeze
hervir	to boil
negar	to deny
perder	to lose
preferir	to prefer
sentir	to feel, be sorry

entender

There are three groups of stem-changing verbs, arranged by the particular spelling change. The verbs in this group have an "o-ue" spelling change in all but the *nosotros* and *vosotros* forms. We'll use *volver* (to return) as a model.

volver—to return

yo	**vuelvo**	nosotros nosotras	**volvemos**
tú	**vuelves**	vosotros vosotras	**volvéis**
él ella Ud.	**vuelve**	ellos ellas Uds.	**vuelven**

Other verbs like *volver*:

acostar	to put (someone) to bed	morir	to die
almorzar	to eat lunch	mostrar	to show
colgar	to hang (up)	poder	to be able, can
costar	to cost	resolver	to solve
dormir	to sleep	torcer	to twist
encontrar	to find, meet	volar	to fly

The third group follows an "e" to "i" spelling change. We'll use *repetir* (to repeat) as a model.

repetir—to repeat

yo	**repito**	nosotros nosotras	**repetimos**
tú	**repites**	vosotros vosotras	**repetís**
él ella Ud.	**repite**	ellos ellas Uds.	**repiten**

Other verbs like *repetir*:

conseguir	to get, obtain (yo consigo)	perseguir	to pursue (yo persigo)
impedir	to stop, impede, prevent	seguir	to follow (yo sigo)
pedir	to ask for, order (food)	vestir	to dress (someone)

Jugar (to play [sports or games]) falls into this category also. The *u* changes to "ue" in the shoe pattern. Here are the forms of *jugar*.

jugar—to play

yo	**juego**	nosotros nosotras	**jugamos**
tú	**juegas**	vosotros vosotras	**jugáis**
él ella Ud.	**juega**	ellos ellas Uds.	**juegan**

jugar

14

Write the *tú* and *nosotros* forms for each verb. Be aware of the spelling changes between the two.

		tú	*nosotros*
2.3	a.	entender	_____	_____
	b.	encender	_____	_____
	c.	defender	_____	_____
	d.	perder	_____	_____
	e.	despertar	_____	_____
	f.	preferir	_____	_____
	g.	fregar	_____	_____
	h.	negar	_____	_____
	i.	confesar	_____	_____
	j.	querer	_____	_____

Change the verb form in the first half of the phrase to agree with the new subject in the second.

2.4   a.   Yo prefiero descansar pero Uds. no _____ descansar.

b.   Mi madre hierve el agua pero tu madre no _____ el agua.

c.   La estudiante entiende la lección pero yo no _____ la lección.

d.   Uds. pierden tiempo pero tú no _____ tiempo.

e.   Nosotros defendemos la patria pero los enemigos no _____ la patria.

f.   Él quiere estudiar pero Uds. no _____ estudiar.

g.   Ellos encienden la luz pero Ud. no _____ la luz.

h.   Yo lo niego pero ellas no lo _____ .

i.   Ella piensa ir pero yo no _____ ir.

Write the forms of the given shoe verb infinitives.

2.5   a.   duermo   (tú) _____   (nosotros) _____

b.   encuentra   (yo) _____   (nosotros) _____

c.   vuela   (nosotros) _____   (ellos) _____

d.   jugamos   (tú) _____   (Ud.) _____

e.   vuelvo   (él) _____   (tú) _____

f. almorzamos   (Ud.) _____   (ellos) _____

g. muere   (tú) _____   (tú y yo) _____

h. pueden   (Chamo) _____   (el equipo) _____

i. colgamos   (yo) _____   (tu amigo) _____

j. tuerce   (Uds.) _____   (Papá) _____

> **Use the given form to change the infinitives of that group to the same form.**

Example: duerme
   a. sonar **suena**
   b. volver **vuelve**
   c. encontrar **encuentra**

2.6   1.   cuelga   a. torcer   b. morir   c. costar

   _____   _____   _____

2.   juegas   a. dormir   b. encontrar   c. acostar

   _____   _____   _____

3.   puedo   a. volver   b. almorzar   c. acostar

   _____   _____   _____

4.   mueres   a. envolver   b. colgar   c. mostrar

   _____   _____   _____

5.   tuerce   a. dormir   b. morir   c. poder

   _____   _____   _____

6.   almuerzan   a. volver   b. resolver   c. contar

   _____   _____   _____

7.   duermen   a. demostrar   b. acostar   c. jugar

   _____   _____   _____

8.   muestra   a. costar   b. volar   c. volver

   _____   _____   _____

9.   acuesto   a. dormir   b. morir   c. poder

   _____   _____   _____

10. muere   a. colgar   b. volar   c. encontrar

   _____   _____   _____

> **Answer these yes/no questions in Spanish. Pay attention to the form change indicated.**

2.7   a.   ¿Puedes tú conducir?

   Sí (No), yo _____

b.   ¿Duermes bien por la noche?

   Sí (No), yo _____

c.   ¿Juega María al béisbol?

   Sí (No), María _____

d. ¿Vuelas a México en el verano?

Sí (No), yo _____

e. ¿Cuentan Uds. el dinero al fin del día?

Sí (No), nosotros _____

f. ¿Encuentran los estudiantes la sala de clase?

Sí (No), ellos _____

g. ¿Demuestro yo el plan ahora?

Sí (No), tú _____

h. ¿Volvemos nosotros a casa a las nueve?

Sí (No), Uds. _____

i. ¿Almuerzas tú en la cafetería?

Sí (No), yo _____

j. ¿Cuelga Ud. la chaqueta?

Sí (No), yo _____

Fill in the missing verb forms for these "e-i" shoe verbs. There is no need for the letter *u* in the *yo* form of *seguir* (*sigo*) or *conseguir* (*consigo*). In Spanish the letter *g* before an *o* is pronounced like the *g* in the English word *go*. The addition of the letter *u* would change the pronunciation. The *g* sound, as in *go*, must be the same in all forms of *seguir* and *conseguir*. The letter *u* is used before *e* or *i*, as in *sigues*, to maintain the *g* sound as in *go*.

2.8 a. sigo, sigues, _____ , _____ seguís, siguen

b. visto, _____ , viste, _____ , vestís, visten

c. _____ , consigues, _____ , _____ , conseguís, consiguen

d. _____ , repites, _____ , repetimos, repetís, _____

e. pido, _____ , _____ , pedimos, pedís, _____

f. _____ , despides, _____ , despedimos, despedís, _____

g. impido, _____ , _____ , _____ , impedís, impiden

Translate these phrases, using the vocabulary (of shoe verbs) from the beginning of the lesson.

2.9 a. I pursue   _____

b. she dresses (the child)   _____

c. you and I stop   _____

d. we repeat   _____

e. the class follows   _____

f. you (Ud.) order   _____

g. you (tú) follow   _____

h. they get _____

i. my friends order _____

 Speaking. Choose five (5) of the activities listed below. Interview a friend as to whether they do them. Your friend will then interview you.

Example: perder el tiempo

(Student 1:) **¿Pierdes el tiempo?**

(Student 2:) **Sí (No), (no) pierdo el tiempo.**

2.10 a. hablar por teléfono

b. mirar la televisión

c. estudiar la tarea

d. jugar al fútbol

e. vivir en un apartamento

f. escribir bien

g. dormir mal

h. beber mucha leche

i. leer la lección

j. volver a casa a tiempo

hablar por teléfono

 Create a dialogue with a partner, using the script below.

2.11 Student 1: suggest an activity for you and your friend

Student 2: refuse the offer, giving an excuse

Student 1: suggest another activity, one that can be done with a group

Student 2: ask who else is going

Student 1: tell who else can do that activity with you two

Student 2: make an alternative suggestion (for an activity)

Student 1: accept the idea

Student 2: give a reason why this is a good idea

✔ Adult check _____

Initial   Date

 Review the material in this section in preparation for the Self Test. This Self Test will check your mastery of this particular section as well as your knowledge of the previous section.

SELF TEST 2

Circle the stem-changing infinitives for each line. (1 pt. each)

2.01 a. seguir   despertar   poner   perder

     b. trabajar   almorzar   repetir   subir

     c. vivir   escribir   cantar   dormir

     d. sentir   pedir   leer   poder

     e. beber   llevar   fregar   pasar

Choose three (3) shoe verbs and three (3) regular verbs. Write their *tú* and *nosotros* forms below. (1 pt. each)

	Infinitive	*tú* form	*nosotros* form
shoe verbs			
2.02 a.	_____	_____	_____
b.	_____	_____	_____
c.	_____	_____	_____
regular verbs			
2.03 a.	_____	_____	_____
b.	_____	_____	_____
c.	_____	_____	_____

Change each form to the one required. Be careful! Stem-changing and regular verbs are mixed! (1 pt. each)

2.04   a. yo defiendo: Uds. _____   f. tú pierdes: ellos _____

     b. Uds. trabajan: nosotros _____   g. ella repite: yo _____

     c. nosotros servimos: tú _____   h. tú lees: las tías _____

     d. la familia trae: tú _____   i. tú y yo dormimos: yo _____

     e. él almuerza: Ud. _____   j. ellos abren: mi hermana _____

Write a ten-sentence composition detailing a typical day in the life of your family. Write five (5) sentences about activities you, your father, sister, etc., do, and five (5) sentences about what you don't do. Use the vocabulary list at the end of the unit, although you're not limited to it. (3 pts. each)

2.05   a. _____

     b. _____

     c. _____

     d. _____

     e. _____

     f. _____

     g. _____

     h. _____

     i. _____

     j. _____

Translate sentences a–e into English. (2 pts. each)

2.06   a.   Duerme mal. _____

        b.   No puedes estudiar en una fiesta. _____

        c.   Pierden dos sombreros. _____

        d.   Describimos la foto. _____

        e.   Abro la puerta para Elena. _____

Translate sentences f–j into Spanish. (2 pts. each)

        f.   We eat lunch in the park. _____

        g.   They live in the city. _____

        h.   I work in an office. _____

        i.   You play hockey. (familiar) _____

        j.   All of you drink coffee. (polite) _____

READING COMPREHENSION.

Read the passage in its entirety first. Then, review the multiple choices for each blank. Read the passage a second time and determine which verb form completes the meaning of each blank. Circle the verb of your choice. (1 pt. each)

2.07   Me gustan los deportes. Es bueno practicar los ejercicios. Por ejemplo, __(1)__ al béisbol. __(2)__ el gimnasio los sábados. Requiere mucho tiempo, pero __(3)__ estar de buena salud. Afortunadamente, no __(4)__ lejos del parque. Cada día, después de la escuela, yo __(5)__ allí.

1. como	2. Pierdo	3. prefiero	4. comprendo	5. camino
vuelvo	Visito	bebo	pido	visto
juego	Hielo	trabajo	vivo	bailo

2.08   Mi hermano tiene muchos pasatiempos. En el verano, cuando hace calor, __(1)__ a la piscina pública. Cuando llueve, __(2)__ novelas. En diciembre __(3)__ películas con sus amigos. Pero, en mayo, __(4)__ en el jardín. De vez en cuando __(5)__ artículos para el periódico.

1. nada	2. busca	3. compra	4. pierde	5. escupe
come	lee	mira	trabaja	vuela
muestra	trae	pide	siente	escribe

2.09   Por la mañana, nos __(1)__ la cara y los dientes. No __(2)__ el desayuno en casa, sino en la cafetería de la escuela. No vamos a la escuela en autobús, sino que __(3)__ . En la clase __(4)__ las tareas. Durante el almuerzo __(5)__ con nuestros amigos.

1. perdemos	2. vivimos	3. podemos	4. hacemos	5. sudamos
volvemos	comemos	caminamos	jugamos	dormimos
lavamos	despedimos	repetimos	abrimos	hablamos

82 / 103

Score _____

Adult Check _____

Initial   Date

III. REVIEW IRREGULAR VERBS OF THE PRESENT TENSE

The final group of verbs reviewed in this chapter are called "irregular." They do not follow the pattern they are supposed to, or have forms that are completely different from the infinitive. Effort must be made to memorize the irregular verb forms.

We shall begin with infinitives that have an irregular *yo* form only. Look at the forms of the verb *salir*.

salir—to leave, go out

yo	**salgo**	nosotros nosotras	**salimos**
tú	**sales**	vosotros vosotras	**salís**
él ella Ud.	**sale**	ellos ellas Uds.	**salen**

3.1 a. How is the *yo* form different? _____

   b. Do any other forms follow that spelling? _____

hacer—to do, make

yo	**hago**	nosotros nosotras	**hacemos**
tú	**haces**	vosotros vosotras	**hacéis**
él ella Ud.	**hace**	ellos ellas Uds.	**hacen**

3.2 a. How is *hacer* similar to *salir*? _____

_____

   b. Are there any other spelling changes in the verb *hacer* _____

Verbs like the two above are nicknamed "yo-go" verbs to help you remember the spelling change.

c. How does the nickname "yo-go" help you remember? _____

There are two more "yo-go" verbs to be reviewed here. Check out the forms of *poner* and *traer*.

poner—to put, place, set

yo	**pongo**	nosotros nosotras	**ponemos**
tú	**pones**	vosotros vosotras	**ponéis**
él ella Ud.	**pone**	ellos ellas Uds.	**ponen**

traer—to bring

yo	**traigo**	nosotros nosotras	**traemos**
tú	**traes**	vosotros vosotras	**traéis**
él ella Ud	**trae**	ellos ellas Uds.	**traen**

d. What additional change occurs in the *yo* form of traer? _____

Basically, the only new material here is the *yo* forms. The rest of the forms are spelled regularly. Since you have already mastered regular verb endings, most of the forms should be easy to deduce. You will have to memorize the *yo* forms only. Before we continue, here are a few review questions.

3.3   a. Of all the forms reviewed above, which means "I do"? _____

b. Which form means "I bring"? _____

c. Which form means "I leave"? _____

d. Which form means "I put"? _____

e. Translate "they make." _____

22

f. Translate "they bring." _____

g. Which form means "you go out"? _____

h. Translate "you set." _____

Continue. Presented here is another group of verbs which have irregular *yo* forms, although they do not fit the "yo-go" nickname. Since only their *yo* form is irregular, we will present only the *yo* and *nosotros* forms here.

escoger (to choose)	yo **escojo**	nosotros **escogemos**
conducir (to drive)	yo **conduzco**	nosotros **conducimos**
conocer (to know [people])	yo **conozco**	nosotros **conocemos**
dar (to give)	yo **doy**	nosotros **damos**
ofrecer (to offer)	yo **ofrezco**	nosotros **ofrecemos**
saber (to know [facts, a skill])	yo **sé**	nosotros **sabemos**
ver (to see)	yo **veo**	nosotros **vemos**

Estar has accents and an irregular *yo* form. These accents are important to the meaning of the particular words, so you have to memorize carefully where they are.

estar—to be

yo	**estoy**	nosotros nosotras	**estamos**
tú	**estás**	vosotros vosotras	**estáis**
él ella Ud.	**está**	ellos ellas Uds.	**están**

Remembering that the rest of the forms are regular, review these verbs.

Complete the following questions.

3.4   a. If *dar* means *to give*, how do you translate "he gives"? _____

b. If *conducir* means *to drive*, how do you translate "they drive"? _____

c. If *estar* means *to be,* how do you translate "you (formal) are"? _____

d. If *ofrecer* means *to offer*, how do you translate "all of you offer"? _____

e. If *saber* means *to know*, how do you translate "she knows"? _____

List what each person would bring to a party, and where he or she places it. Use the forms of *traer* (to bring) and *poner* (to put).

Example: Yo/los platos/en la cocina
Yo traigo los platos. Pongo los platos en la cocina.

3.5   a.   Ellos/las frutas/en la cocina

_____

b.   María/la leche/en el refrigerador

_____

c.   Nosotros/el café/en el comedor

_____

d.   Ustedes/los sandwiches/en la mesa

_____

e.   Tú y Carlos/los refrescos/en el garaje

_____

f.   Las muchachas/un radio/en el sótano

_____

g.   Tú/los tenedores/a la izquierda de los platos

_____

h.   Raúl y yo/los vasos/en el gabinete

_____

i.   La familia/los dulces/en un plato hondo (a bowl)

_____

Answer each question in a complete Spanish sentence with *yo*.

3.6   a.   ¿Quién conduce ese coche?

_____

b.   ¿Quién ve la película?

_____

c.   ¿Quién conoce a Juana?

_____

d.   ¿Quién está aquí?

_____

e.   ¿Quién pone la mesa?

_____

f.   ¿Quién escoge los libros?

_____

g. ¿Quién hace la tarea?

_____

h. ¿Quién da el dinero a Elena?

_____

i. ¿Quién sale a las ocho?

_____

j. ¿Quién trae un lápiz a la clase?

_____

Finally, we will review the truly irregular verbs. These forms *must* be memorized.

ir—to go

yo	**voy**	nosotros nosotras	**vamos**
tú	**vas**	vosotros vosotras	**vais**
él ella Ud.	**va**	ellos ellas Uds.	**van**

3.7 a. Which form means "We are going"? _____

b. Which form means "He is going"? _____

c. Translate *yo voy* three different ways. _____

ser—to be

yo	**soy**	nosotros nosotras	**somos**
tú	**eres**	vosotros vosotras	**sois**
él ella Ud.	**es**	ellos ellas Uds.	**son**

Answer the following questions.

3.8   a.   Which form means "I am"? _____

        b.   Which form means "They are"? _____

        c.   Translate *Nosotros somos.* _____

tener—to have

yo	**tengo**	nosotros nosotras	**tenemos**
tú	**tienes**	vosotros vosotras	**tenéis**
él ella Ud.	**tiene**	ellos ellas Uds.	**tienen**

 Answer the following questions.

3.9   a.   Which form means "you (informal) have"? _____

        b.   Which form means "all of you have"? _____

        c.   Translate *¿Ud. tiene…?* _____

venir—to come

yo	**vengo**	nosotros nosotras	**venimos**
tú	**vienes**	vosotros vosotras	**venís**
él ella Ud.	**viene**	ellos ellas Uds.	**vienen**

 Answer the following questions.

3.10   a.   Translate *venimos* in three different ways. _____

        b.   Translate *vengo* in three different ways. _____

        c.   Which form means "you are coming"? _____

decir—to say, tell

yo	**digo**	nosotros nosotras	**decimos**
tú	**dices**	vosotros vosotras	**decís**
él ella Ud.	**dice**	ellos ellas Uds.	**dicen**

Answer the following questions.

3.11　a.　Translate *ellos no dicen* in two different ways. _____

　　　　b.　Translate *dices* in three different ways. _____

　　　　c　Which form means "I am telling"? _____

oír—to hear

yo	**oigo**	nosotros nosotras	**oímos**
tú	**oyes**	vosotros vosotras	**oís**
él ella Ud.	**oye**	ellos ellas Uds.	**oyen**

Answer the following questions.

3.12　a.　Which form means "you (formal) are hearing"? _____

　　　　b.　Which form means "I hear"? _____

　　　　c.　Translate *ellas oyen* in three different ways. _____

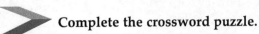
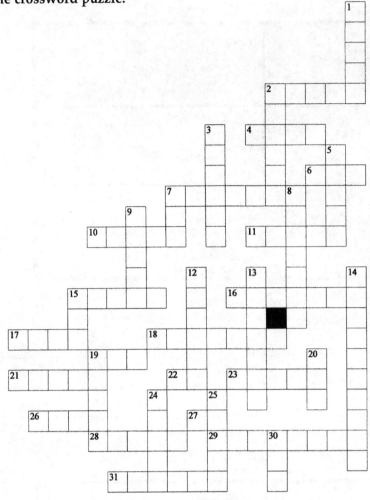

ACROSS

2. traer (tú)
4. hacer (ella)
6. dar (tú)
7. venir (nosotros)
10. traer (ellos)
11. saber (tú)
15. ver (nosotros)
16. conocer (yo)
17. ser (tú)
18. tener (nosotros)
19. ser (ellos)
21. venir (yo)
22. ser (él)
23. tener (yo)
26. hacer (yo)
27. ir (él)
28. salir (Uds.)
29. conducir (yo)
31. tener (tú)

DOWN

1. ir (nosotros)
2. traer (yo)
3. tener (Uds.)
5. salir (tú)
7. ir (ellos)
8. saber (nosotros)
9. salir (yo)
12. venir (tú)
13. conocer (tú)
14. conducir (nosotros)
15. ir (tú)
19. ser (nosotros)
20. dar (yo)
24. tener (ella)
25. hacer (tú)
30. dar (Uds.)

 Change the given *ellos* forms to *yo* forms. Then, change those *yo* forms to *tú* forms.

	yo	tú
3.14 a. son		
b. tienen		
c. van		
d. vienen		
e. dicen		

Translate the phrases into Spanish. Use the irregular verbs.

3.15   a.   he is   _____

       b.   we don't come   _____

       c.   they have   _____

       d.   you go   _____

       e.   I am saying   _____

       f.   all of you are   _____

       g.   we aren't   _____

       h.   you say   _____

       i.   she goes   _____

       j.   I don't have   _____

Quiz your grammar knowledge. Read the following passages and answer the true/false questions for each. Look for clues in the grammar, as they will help you as much as actually translating. Choose *t* for *true*, *f* for *false* and *u* for *unable to tell*.

3.16   a.   Caminas para la buena salud. Estudias mucho. Tienes mucho éxito. Eres popular.

            _____   The subject is male.

            _____   The subject is rather busy.

            _____   The subject is female.

       b.   Estoy ocupada todos los días. Trabajo en un hospital. Me gusta. Conozco a muchas personas.

            _____   The subject is female.

            _____   The subject could be a doctor.

            _____   The subject would like to change careers.

       c.   Tenemos una familia grande. Hay mis padres y cinco hermanas. Soy el único chico. Nos gustan los animales. Dos perros y tres gatos viven en mi casa. ¡Cuesta mucho darnos de comer!

            _____   This family has many pets.

            _____   This person is an only child.

            _____   This family has a large grocery bill.

       d.   Juegan al béisbol. Participan en el equipo de la escuela. Practican todos los días. Marcan más puntos que los otros equipos. Son campeones.

            _____   They like school.

            _____   They practice a lot.

            _____   They have a losing record.

e. Escribe poesía. Es autor. Trabaja en casa. Recibe algunos premios por su poesía. Va a muchas universidades para presentar sus obras.

_____ This passage is about a group of people.

_____ The subject is successful.

_____ The subject is a college professor.

 Practice writing. Choose one of the following pictures. Write a ten-sentence composition narrating a STORY about that picture. Try to avoid too much description; discuss the actions.

Picture 1

Picture 2

3.17 _____

_____

_____

_____

_____

_____

_____

_____

_____

_____

_____

_____

_____

✔ Adult check _____

Initial   Date

Exercise 1. Choose who performs the activity by listening to the verb form. Circle the correct response. [CD–A, Track 1]

1. a. Elena y yo   b. tú   c. Uds.
2. a. Uds.   b. Ud.   c. ella
3. a. la familia   b. tú   c. yo
4. a. tú y yo   b. Conchita   c. tú
5. a. a mí   b. Raúl   c. yo
6. a. tú   b. nosotros   c. la familia
7. a. la hermana   b. las hermanas c. Beto
8. a. yo   b. Uds.   c. nosotros
9. a. María   b. tú y yo   c. Uds.
10. a. Uds.   b. mi familia   c. Uds. y yo

Exercise 2. Match the activity described to its picture. [CD–A, Track 2]

1. _____   6. _____
2. _____   7. _____
3. _____   8. _____
4. _____   9. _____
5. _____   10. _____

a   b   c

d

e

f

g

h

i

j

 Review the material in this section in preparation for the Self Test. This Self Test will check your mastery of this particular section as well as your knowledge of all previous sections.

SELF TEST 3

Write the correct *yo* form of the following verbs. (1 pt. each)

3.01 a. hacer _____

   b. traer _____

   c. conducir _____

   d. saber _____

   e. dar _____

   f. poner _____

   g. escoger _____

   h. salir _____

   i. ir _____

   j. oír _____

Answer the following questions in complete Spanish sentences. (3 pts. each)

3.02 a. ¿Qué trae Pedro a la fiesta?

    _____

   b. ¿Quién hace la tarea todos los días?

    _____

   c. ¿Va Ud. a la casa de Carlos todos los sábados?

    _____

   d. ¿Tienen Uds. mucha tarea en la clase de matemáticas?

    _____

   e. ¿A qué hora sales de tu casa para ir a la iglesia?

    _____

   f. ¿Siempre dices la verdad?

    _____

Write the correct forms of the following verbs. (1 pt. each blank)

3.03 a. estar

    ella _____ Uds. _____

   b. tener

    yo _____ ellos _____

c. decir

   tú _____   nosotros _____

d. poner

   yo _____   nosotros _____

e. ver

   ellos _____   yo _____

f. escoger

   tú _____   Uds. _____

g. saber

   Ud. _____   yo _____

h. ofrecer

   yo _____   nosotros _____

i. ser

   tú _____   Uds. _____

j. estar

   ella _____   yo _____

Circle the correct verb form for each sentence. (1 pt. each)

3.04   a. Uds. (tienen / vienen) a la fiesta de María Luisa.

       b. Nosotros (decimos / damos) los libros a la profesora.

       c. Yo (soy / veo) un perro en la casa de mis amigos.

       d. Tú y yo (conducimos / traemos) los lápices a la biblioteca.

       e. Roberto (oye / va) la música clásica.

       f. Las muchachas (ofrecen / ponen) los platos en la mesa.

       g. Nosotros (conocemos / sabemos) a la tía de José.

       h. ¿Qué (sales / haces) el domingo por la mañana?

       i. Ud. (es / va) a la tienda para comprar zapatos.

       j. Ellas (oyen / escogen) los colores de los platos nuevos.

IV. REVIEW NUMBERS 0–1,000,000

A.   **Use this list as a reference to review the numbers in Spanish.**

0	cero		21	veintiuno
1	uno (un, una)		30	treinta
2	dos		31	treinta y uno
3	tres		40	cuarenta
4	cuatro		50	cincuenta
5	cinco		60	sesenta
6	seis		70	setenta
7	siete		80	ochenta
8	ocho		90	noventa
9	nueve		100	cien (ciento)
10	diez		200	doscientos(as)
11	once		300	trescientos(as)
12	doce		400	cuatrocientos(as)
13	trece		500	quinientos(as)
14	catorce		600	seiscientos(as)
15	quince		700	setecientos(as)
16	dieciséis		800	ochocientos(as)
17	diecisiete		900	novecientos(as)
18	dieciocho		1,000	mil
19	diecinueve		10, 000	diez mil
20	veinte		100,000	cien mil
			1,000,000	un millón

> **Look closely at numbers 16–19.**

4.1   a.   Translate "sixteen" word for word in Spanish. _____

You can see the pattern evolve from there.

b.   Translate "nineteen." _____

c.   How does the word *y* translate? _____

The number twenty-one was provided to suggest the pattern of number formation for the rest of the numbers up to 100. Observing how the pattern holds, and the whole tens, you can easily count up to 100.

d.   Translate 46 (*cuarenta y seis*) word for word. _____

e.   Translate 93 (*noventa y tres*) word for word. _____

> **Now you have the idea! Write the following numbers in Spanish.**

4.2   a.   75 _____

b.   82 _____

c.   29 _____

d.   68 _____

e.   47 _____

B. Only the "hundreds" agree in gender with the noun they modify. Look at the examples:

Trescientos señores

Trescientas señoritas

C. If *mil* is used to express a specific quantity, it does not change.

Hay cinco mil personas en el concierto.

There are 5,000 people at the concert.

However, use *miles* (thousands) to express a general quantity.

Hay miles de kilómetros entre México y Nueva York.

There are thousands of kilometers between Mexico and New York.

D. Use *cien* anytime you can write the numeral 100.

100.000—cien mil

1.100.352—un millón cien mil trescientos cincuenta y dos

Use *ciento* for any amount over 100.

164—ciento sesenta y cuatro

103—ciento tres

112—ciento doce

E. Use *un millón, dos millones, tres millones...* to express a numeric quantity.

4.873.067—cuatro millones ochocientos setenta y tres mil sesenta y siete

1.463.111—un millón cuatrocientos sesenta y tres mil ciento once

Use *un millón de* or *millones de* when describing a quantity of specific things.

Había tres millones de coches fabricados en esa fábrica.

There were three million cars made in that factory.

Parece que hay un millón de estrellas en el cielo.

It seems there are a million stars in the sky.

F. When expressing one of any given item, use the indefinite articles *un* and *una* instead of the numeral *uno*.

una semana—one week

Hay un chico—There's one boy.

Phone numbers may be given as individual digits or grouped in segments of two numbers.

Example: 7 - 82 - 43 - 81

Write out each phone number in Spanish in segments like the example above.

4.3   a.   782-4381   _____

        b.   598-6001   _____

        c.   607-2549   _____

        d.   418-8410   _____

        e.   200-6413   _____

f.   888-1264   _____

g.   your own   _____

h.   a friend's   _____

✔ Adult check _____

                                           Initial   Date

MENU

LAS BEBIDAS

Un café	7 pesos
Una Coca-Cola	12 pesos

LOS PLATOS

Una hamburguesa	44 pesos
El pollo frito...	66 pesos

LOS ACOMPANAMIENTOS

Las papas fritas	28 pesos
Una ensalada..	33 pesos

LOS POSTRES

El helado	37 pesos
La tarta de cereza.................................	49 pesos

➤ **Total each order and write the bill in Spanish.**

4.4   a.   un café, un pollo, un helado   _____

          b.   una Coca-Cola, una ensalada   _____

          c.   una Coca-Cola, una hamburguesa,
              las papas fritas   _____

          d.   un café, un helado   _____

          e.   un helado, una tarta de cereza   _____

          f.   una Coca-Cola, un helado   _____

➤ **Write the numerals.**

4.5   a.   setecientos cuarenta y cinco   _____

          b.   novecientos diecisiete   _____

          c.   mil ciento seis   _____

          d.   doscientos   _____

          e.   quinientos veintiocho   _____

          f.   noventa y nueve   _____

g. novecientos nueve   _____

h. seiscientos treinta   _____

i. dos mil cuatrocientos cincuenta y cinco   _____

j. un millón trescientos mil once   _____

▶ **Write out each year in Spanish.**

4.6   a.   1972   _____

      b.   1999   _____

      c.   1981   _____

      d.   1878   _____

      e.   1654   _____

      f.   1901   _____

      g.   1477   _____

      h.   1967   _____

      i.   1814   _____

      j.   2007   _____

IMPROVE YOUR READING COMPREHENSION.

Below is a spreadsheet detailing the weekly and monthly salaries (*sueldos*) of the employees of a particular company. Use the spreadsheet to answer the questions below.

NOMBRE	SUELDO SEMANAL	SUELDO MENSUAL
J. Muñoz	250	1.000
M. de Rivera	98	392
R. Alabeña	150	600
E. Sobejano	410	1.640
C. Rodríguez	321	1.284
A. de Matas	511	2.044
T. Tiburón	279	1.116
S. Barga	636	2.544

Answer the questions in complete Spanish sentences, writing out all numbers.

4.7 a.   ¿Cuánto gana la Sra. de Rivera por mes?

_____

b.   ¿Cuánta gana el Sr. Tiburón por semana?

_____

c.   ¿Cuánto gana la Sra. Barga por mes?

_____

d.   ¿Cuánto gana el Sr. Alabeña por semana?

_____

e.   ¿Es verdad que la Sra. de Matas gana dos mil cuarenta y cuatro dólares por mes? Si no es verdad, ¿cuánta gana? _____

f.   ¿Gana el Sr. Muñoz más por semana que la Sra. de Rivera? ¿Cuánto gana cada persona?

_____

g.   ¿Quién gana trescientos noventa y dos dólares por mes?

_____

✔ Adult check _____

Initial   Date

Review the material in this section in preparation for the Self Test. This Self Test will check your mastery of this particular section as well as your knowledge of all previous sections.

SELF TEST 4

4.01   **Match.** (1 pt. each)

1.	_____	cien	a.	500
2.	_____	setenta	b.	10
3.	_____	quinientos	c.	900
4.	_____	diez	d.	100
5.	_____	noventa	e.	90
6.	_____	trescientos	f.	101
7.	_____	cincuenta	g.	80
8.	_____	seiscientos	h.	700
9.	_____	cuarenta	i.	50
10.	_____	ochocientos	j.	200
11	_____	veinte	k.	1.000
12.	_____	mil	l.	30
13.	_____	ciento uno	m.	600
14.	_____	treinta	n.	400
15.	_____	novecientos	o.	20
16.	_____	ochenta	p.	70
17.	_____	sesenta	q.	800
18.	_____	cuatrocientos	r.	40
19.	_____	doscientos	s.	300
20.	_____	setecientos	t.	60

4.02   **Choose the number that correctly completes each math problem.** (1 pt. each)

1. ochenta y tres + nueve = _____
    a. doce
    b. noventa y dos
    c. novecientos dos

2. mil setecientos + _____ = mil setecientos
    cincuenta y seis
    a. cinco
    b. ciento seis
    c. cincuenta y seis

3. _____ – veintiuno = ciento treinta y cuatro
    a. ciento cincuenta y cinco
    b. cinco mil
    c. cuarenta y cuatro

4. quince x tres = _____
    a. cuatrocientos cuarenta y cinco
    b. cuarenta y cinco
    c. doce

5. ciento veintiséis + _____ = mil
    a. ochocientos cuarenta y cinco
    b. ochenta y cuatro
    c. ochocientos setenta y cuatro

8. cincuenta y seis – cuarenta y tres = _____
    a. tres
    b. trece
    c. treinta y tres

6. _____ – quinientos ocho = trescientos noventa y nueve
    a. novecientos siete
    b. mil siete
    c. diecisiete

9. mil quinientos ochenta y uno + _____ = dos mil quinientos ochenta y uno
    a. un millón
    b. cien
    c. mil

7. seis x doce = _____
    a. sesenta y dos
    b. doce
    c. setenta y dos

10. _____ – sesenta y dos = setecientos quince
    a. siete
    b. dieciséis
    c. setecientos setenta y siete

4.03   **Complete the translations. Be mindful of which numbers agree in gender with the nouns given. Some answers may require more than one word.** (1 pt. each)

a.	75 people	_____	personas
b.	102 pages	_____	páginas
c.	1.015 seats	_____	asientos
d.	200 ladies	_____	señoras
e.	1,000 dollars	_____	dólares
f.	82 days	_____	días
g.	764 insects	_____	insectos
h.	one month	_____	mes
i.	6.240 homes	_____	casas
j.	100 problems	_____	problemas
k.	13 cents	_____	centavos
l.	a million prizes	_____	premios
m.	538 rooms	_____	cuartos
n.	999 puppies	_____	perritos
o.	one woman	_____	mujer

V. REVIEW DATES AND TELLING TIME

DAYS OF THE WEEK IN SPANISH

lunes	Monday
martes	Tuesday
miércoles	Wednesday
jueves	Thursday
viernes	Friday
sábado	Saturday
domingo	Sunday

Please note that the days of the week **are not** capitalized in Spanish. It is also important to remember that the Spanish calendar runs from Monday to Sunday.

MONTHS OF THE YEAR IN SPANISH

enero	January
febrero	February
marzo	March
abril	April
mayo	May
junio	June
julio	July
agosto	August
septiembre	September
octubre	October
noviembre	November
diciembre	December

Please note that Spanish speakers **do not** capitalize the months either.

SUPPLEMENTAL VOCABULARY

hoy es	today is	el año	the year
mañana es	tomorrow is	el primero	the first
ayer fue	yesterday was	el mes	the month
el día	the day	la semana	the week
la fecha	the date		

Now, think about HOW the date is expressed in Spanish. How would an English speaker express the following date: **6/8/92**

English speakers think June 8, 1992.

However, the date is expressed differently in Spanish.

> **Example: El ocho de junio de mil novecientos noventa y dos.**

5.1   a.   Translate it word for word. _____

  b.   How is that different from your first impression? _____

It is important when expressing the date in Spanish to invert the date and month, even when abbreviating.

  c.   In Spanish, abbreviate the above date. _____

When expressing dates in Spanish, use "primero" for the first, and then use the regular cardinal numbers (*dos, tres, cuatro*...) for the rest of the month. First, abbreviate the English date; second, write that date in Spanish (longhand); and third, abbreviate the date as a Spanish speaker would. Follow the example.

	July 18	7/18	el dieciocho de julio	18/7
5.2 a.	October 15	_____	_____	_____
b.	June 2	_____	_____	_____
c.	March 30	_____	_____	_____
d.	August 1	_____	_____	_____
e.	November 10	_____	_____	_____

Read the dates given. Write what the date would have been the day before the one given. Begin each response with the phrase *ayer fue* from the supplemental vocabulary.

5.3   a.   Hoy es lunes, el ocho de diciembre.

  _____

  b.   Hoy es jueves, el veinticinco de agosto.

  _____

  c.   Hoy es sábado, el dieciséis de febrero.

  _____

  d.   Hoy es domingo, el dos de enero.

  _____

  e.   Hoy es viernes, el veinte de septiembre.

  _____

  f.   Hoy es martes, el treinta y uno de marzo.

  _____

g. Hoy es miércoles, el diez de julio.

_____

h. Hoy es sábado, el cinco de mayo.

_____

i. Hoy es lunes, el veintitrés de noviembre.

_____

j. Hoy es miércoles, el diecinueve de junio.

_____

 Write the date of the following holidays in Spanish.

5.4

a.

_____

_____

_____

b.

_____

_____

_____

c.

_____

_____

_____

d.

_____

_____

_____

e.

_____

_____

_____

f.

_____

_____

_____

g.

_____
_____
_____

h.

_____
_____
_____

i.

_____
_____
_____

j.

_____
_____
_____

> **Translate into Spanish.**

5.5   a.   Today is Friday, June 5.

_____

b.   Yesterday was Monday, February 1.

_____

c.   Today is Sunday, March 28.

_____

d.   Tomorrow is Thursday, April 26.

_____

e.   Tomorrow is Tuesday, December 24.

_____

f.	Yesterday was Saturday, July 13.

_____

g.	Tomorrow is Wednesday, October 2.

_____

h.	Today is Thursday, January 14.

_____

i.	Today is Monday, September 30.

_____

j.	Yesterday was Friday, August 1, 2007.

_____

Write the birthdays of those with whom you live. Read your paragraph out loud.

5.6	_____

_____

_____

_____

✔ Adult check _____

TELLING TIME

¿Qué hora es?					¿Qué hora es?

Son las cuatro.					Son las nueve.

Using the visual cues provided, translate each.

5.7	a.	¿Qué hora es?			_____

b.	Translate *son las cuatro*.			_____

c.	Translate *son las nueve*.			_____

d.	How does each sentence begin?		_____

e.	How is each expression ended?		_____

Translate into Spanish.

5.8	a.	It's eight o'clock.			_____

b.	It's eleven o'clock.			_____

c.	It's three o'clock.			_____

Generally, the rule is begin with *son las* and add on the number of the hour. However, there is one exception.

¿Qué hora es?

Es la una.

When the time begins with one o'clock, it is expressed as *es la*. Read the following:

¿Qué hora es?

Son las siete y
veinticinco.

¿Qué hora es?

Es la una y cuarto.

¿Qué hora es?

Son las diez y media.

Note: Be careful not to mix up *cuatro* and *cuarto*!

It's obvious that the clocks read 7:25 and 1:15. Translating word for word, however, helps understand how the system of telling time works. "It's 7:25" in Spanish is really expressed as "It's seven o'clock and twenty five (minutes)."

5.9 1. Translate *Son las ocho y veinticinco.* _____

2. Translate *Son las ocho y cinco.* _____

Observe the second clock. The expression reads 1:15, but we know the word for fifteen is *quince*.

3. a. To what English time expression is *cuarto* closely related? _____

b. Translate *Es la una y cuarto* word for word. _____

c. Now that you can say "It's 1:15," try "It's 3:15." _____

d. "It's 5:15." _____

Observe the third clock. We know "thirty" to be *treinta,* but here a different term has been used.

4. What English expression is equivalent to *y media*? _____

If *Son las diez y media* is "It's 10:30," how would you translate the following?

5. a. "It's 4:30"? _____

b. "It's 12:30"? _____

*It's interesting to note with the advent of digital clocks, it has become acceptable in Spanish-speaking countries to express the quarter hour as *quince* and the half hour as *y treinta*. So you may use *Es la una y quince,* or *Son las seis y treinta*, if you wish. It is wise to choose the expression you prefer and stay with that one (in order to avoid confusion and mistakes).

In Spanish, if the minute hand is past the half hour mark (:30), the time is read with the next hour minus the number of minutes before that hour. For example, observe the following clock:

In English, the time would read, "ten fifty-eight" or 10:58. In Spanish, it would literally read "eleven minus two (minutes)" or "*Son las once menos dos.*" Following are three more clocks to complete this discussion on telling time in Spanish

¿Qué hora es?	¿Qué hora es?	¿Qué hora es?

Son las tres menos diez.	Son las cuatro menos veintitrés.	Es la una menos cuarto.

Our first clock reads 2:50.

5.10   a.   Translate the Spanish for 2:50. _____

b.   Translate the the Spanish for 3:37. _____

c.   Translate the Spanish for 12:45. _____

5.11   Explain the process. _____

It almost feels as if one were going counter-clockwise to read the time. Figure out the minutes remaining until the next whole hour.

> **Express.**

5.12   a.   10:38   _____

b.   7:50   _____

c.   2:45   _____

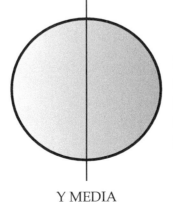

To sum up:
If the LONG hand is on the LEFT side of the clock, use *son las/es la* and go to NEXT whole hour. Then use *menos* and the remaining minutes until the hour.

If the LONG hand is on the RIGHT side of the clock, use *son las/es la* and the SAME whole hour. Then use *y* and the number of minutes AFTER the hour.

Y MEDIA

SUPPLEMENTAL VOCABULARY

¿A qué hora?—At what time?

a eso de…—at about…

a tiempo—on time

de la noche—P.M. (five o'clock until 11:59)

en punto—on the dot, exactly

temprano—early

¿Cuándo?—When?

a las/a la…—at …o'clock

de la mañana—A.M.

de la tarde—P.M. (noon until five o'clock)

tarde—late

medianoche—midnight

mediodía—noon

> **Fill in the blanks in order to complete the translations.**

5.13   a.   It's 3:15.   Son las _____ .

     b.   It's 6:45.   _____ siete menos cuarto.

     c.   It's 5:10 A.M.   Son las _____ y diez _____ .

     d.   It's 1:01.   _____ una y uno.

     e.   at 7:11   _____ siete y once

     f.   It's midnight.   Es _____ .

     g.   It's 4:45.   Son las _____ cuarto.

     h.   It's 12:00 noon.   Es _____ .

     i.   It's 8:30 P.M.   Son las ocho y _____ .

     j.   at 2:09 P.M.   a las dos _____ nueve _____

> **Translate into English. Use the supplemental vocabulary to help you.**

5.14   a.   Son las seis y media.   _____

     b.   Es la una menos diez.   _____

     c.   La fiesta es a eso de las nueve.   _____

     d.   Es medianoche en punto.   _____

     e.   Son las once menos veinticinco
        de la mañana.   _____

     f.   A las diez y catorce de la noche.   _____

     g.   ¿Qué hora es?   _____

     h.   Son las ocho y media.   _____

     i.   A las dos menos cuarto en punto.   _____

     j.   ¿A qué hora es la clase?   _____

Answer the questions in Spanish, with the correct time, specifying A.M. or P.M. Be careful of the change of verb form from question to answer.

Example: ¿Cuándo te despiertas?

(Yo) me despierto a las seis y media de la mañana.

5.15 a. ¿Cuándo vas a la escuela? (8:00)

_____

b. ¿Cuándo te duermes? (11:00)

_____

c. ¿Cuándo juegas al vólibol? (4:00)

_____

d. ¿Cuándo vienes al gimnasio? (1:00)

_____

e. ¿A qué hora hablas con tus amigos? (12:00)

_____

f. ¿A qué hora comes la cena? (6:00)

_____

g. ¿A qué hora quieres ir a casa? (3:15)

_____

h. ¿ A qué hora haces la tarea? (7:30)

_____

i. ¿A qué hora sales de la escuela? (3:45)

_____

j. ¿A qué hora te acuestas? (10:00)

_____

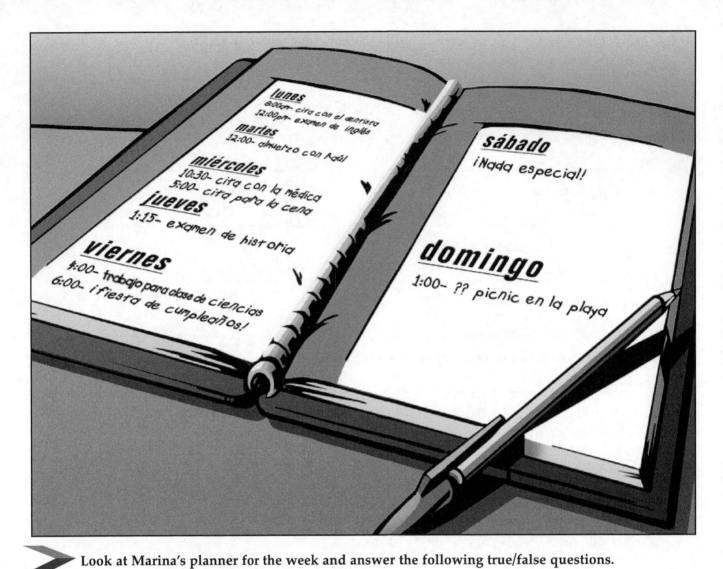

lunes
8:00am- cita con el dentista
12:00pm- examen de inglés

martes
12:00- almuerzo con Raúl

miércoles
10:30- cita con la médica
5:00- cita para la cena

jueves
1:15- examen de historia

viernes
4:00- trabajo para clase de ciencias
6:00- ¡fiesta de cumpleaños!

sábado
¡Nada especial!

domingo
1:00- ?? picnic en la playa

▶ Look at Marina's planner for the week and answer the following true/false questions.
Write *v* for *verdadero* and *f* for *falso*.

5.16   a. _____   Marina has a history exam Friday at 1:00.

        b. _____   Marina is going to a picnic Sunday at 12:00.

        c. _____   Marina is going to a party on Friday at 6:00.

        d. _____   Marina has a Spanish exam Thursday at 1:00.

        e. _____   Marina is going out Wednesday night at 5:00.

▶ Write the date and time of the following events in Marina's life. You may answer in English.

5.17   a. a science paper is due   _____

        b. a lunch date   _____

        c. a doctor's appointment   _____

        d. a totally free day   _____

        e. an English test   _____

SPANISH II

UNIT 1

LIFEPAC TEST

108 / 135

Name _____

Date _____

Score _____

SPANISH II LIFEPAC TEST UNIT 1

1. **Match each sentence to the correct picture.** (1 pt. each)

1. _____ Ella lee a las ocho de la noche.

2. _____ El equipo juega al vólibol a las tres.

3. _____ La secretaria trabaja en la oficina a las diez y media.

4. _____ Yo como un sandwich a las doce y veinte.

5. _____ Estudias conmigo a las cuatro menos veinte en la biblioteca.

6. _____ Es necesario ponerme el traje a las nueve menos cuarto.

7. _____ A ellos les gusta beber refrescos con la cena a las seis y diez.

8. _____ Mi bebé no duerme bien a medianoche.

9. _____ Acabamos de ganar a la una.

10. _____ Los hermanos se afeitan a las siete y media.

a.

b.

c.

d.

e.

f.

g.

h.

i.

j.

2. **Circle the letter of the sentence that best describes the picture.** (1 pt. each)

a. Está contenta.

b. Está aburrida.

c. Está triste.

d. Está estudiando.

a. Estamos sorprendidos.

b. Estamos aburridos.

c. Estamos jugando.

d. Estamos contentos.

a. Somos hermanos.

b. Somos un equipo de vólibol.

c. Estamos tristes.

d. Somos mujeres.

a. Es un equipo de vólibol.

b. Soy rubio.

c. Eres secreteria.

d. Soy joven.

a. ¡Estoy sorprendida!

b. ¡Me lavo las manos!

c. ¡Estoy dormida!

d. ¡Estoy enferma!

3. **Rewrite each sentence with the new subject given, making any necessary changes.** (1 pt. each)

a. La señorita baila el tango. Los hombres y las mujeres

_____

b. Mis primos quieren hablar. Yo

_____

c. Elena sale a las cinco en punto. Tú

_____

d. Ud. escribe una tarea muy larga. Uds.

_____

e. Yo no le doy las gracias a la cajera. Consuelo

_____

f. Tú tienes trece años. Nosotros

_____

g. Los alumnos están caminando al museo. El profesor

_____

h. Me miro en el espejo antes de salir. Tu padre

_____

i. Son mexicanos. Tú

_____

j. Jugamos al tenis los domingos. Tus amigas

_____

Change the given simple present tense forms to the *yo* and *nosotros* forms of the present progressive.
(1 pt. each blank)

			yo	nosotros
4.	a.	hablo	_____	_____
	b.	te afeitas	_____	_____
	c.	cubren	_____	_____
	d.	comprendes	_____	_____
	e.	doy	_____	_____
	f.	te pones	_____	_____
	g.	dormimos	_____	_____

5. **Is the statement true or false? Write _v_ (verdadero) or _f_ (falso). Correct each false sentence.** (1 pt. each)

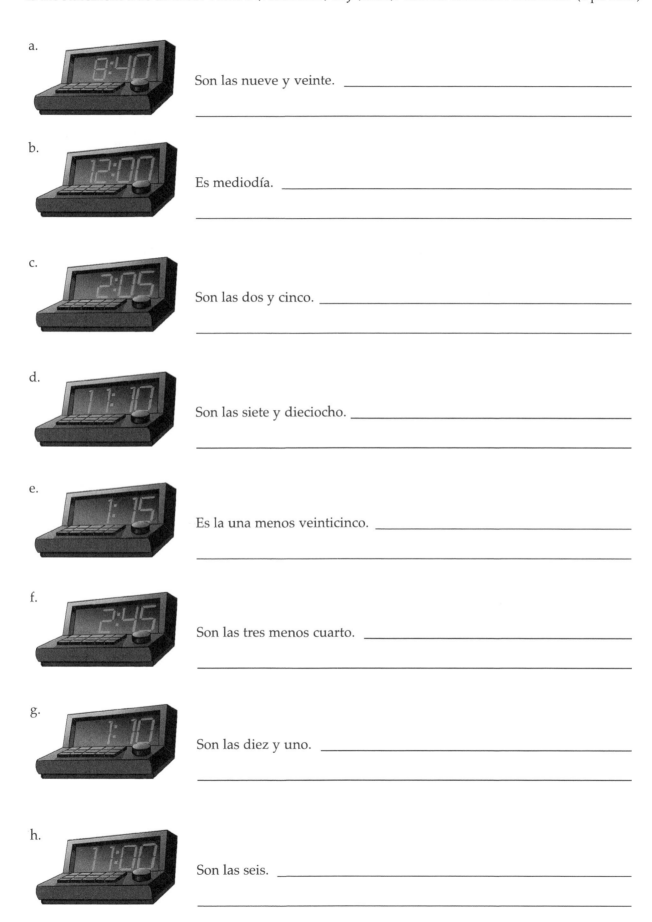

a. Son las nueve y veinte. _____

_____

b. Es mediodía. _____

_____

c. Son las dos y cinco. _____

_____

d. Son las siete y dieciocho. _____

_____

e. Es la una menos veinticinco. _____

_____

f. Son las tres menos cuarto. _____

_____

g. Son las diez y uno. _____

_____

h. Son las seis. _____

_____

i.

Son las siete menos veinticuatro. _____

_____

j.

Son las doce y diez. _____

_____

6.   **Write the responses to the math problems. Write out all numbers in Spanish.** (2 pts. each)

a.   15 x 10 =   _____

b.   250 + 49 =   _____

c.   1,000 – 300 =   _____

d.   426 + 574 =   _____

e.   75 – 19 =   _____

f.   115 + 720 =   _____

g.   100 + 800 =   _____

h.   104 – 8 =   _____

i.   13 + 60 =   _____

j.   1,001 – 900 =   _____

7.   **Write the numerals.** (1 pt. each)

a.   mil setecientos uno   _____

b.   cuatrocientos sesenta y siete   _____

c.   diez mil   _____

d.   quinientos ochenta y cinco   _____

e.   ciento catorce   _____

f.   dos mil trescientos cuarenta y tres   _____

g.   setecientos noventa y nueve   _____

h.   cincuenta   _____

i.   ciento setenta y ocho   _____

j.   novecientos trece   _____

5

8. **Answer each question, based on the cues provided. Use the simple present tense.** (2 pts. each)

   a. ¿Quién juega al básquetbol? (Carlos y Jorge) _____

   b. ¿Quién se lava? (yo) _____

   c. ¿Quién pone la mesa? (él) _____

   d. ¿Quién está aburrido? (Margarita) _____

   e. ¿Quién va al centro? (Uds.) _____

   Answer the questions in the same manner, but use the present progressive verb form. (2 pts. each)

   f. ¿Quién se acuesta? (mis hermanos)

   _____

   g. ¿Quién se divierte mucho? (tú y yo)

   _____

   h. ¿Quién se despierta temprano? (mi padre y yo)

   _____

   i. ¿Quién sirve las bebidas? (los camareros)

   _____

   j. ¿Quién no duerme toda la noche? (yo)

   _____

9. **Calculate the date of the events based on the information given. Write that date in Spanish. You may write the numeral for the day of the month.** (1 pt. each)

   a. Hoy es el quince de abril. Mi cumpleaños viene en diez días. Mi cumpleaños es

   _____

   b. Hoy es el treinta y uno de julio. Se van de vacaciones en dieciocho días. Se van

   _____

   c. Hoy es el primero de febrero. Su aniversario viene en una semana. Su aniversario es

   _____

   d. Hoy es el once de septiembre. Las clases empiezan mañana. Empiezan

   _____

   e. Hoy es el cuatro de enero. Hace cinco días (five days ago) que te hablé. Hablamos (We talked)

   _____

   f. Hoy es el doce de octubre. Celebramos su aniversario en once días. Celebramos

   _____

   g. Hoy es el diecinueve de junio. Hace un mes que nos encontramos (we met). Nos encontramos

   _____

   h. Hoy es el dos de julio. Hace veinticuatro horas que empecé (I began) la tarea. Empecé

   _____

10. **Write the dates out in Spanish. The dates are given in the English style. You may leave the year in numerals.** (2 pts. each)

a. 6/12/99 _____

b. 1/11/98 _____

c. 11/1/2007 _____

d. 7/30/96 _____

e. 3/15/90 _____

f. 10/9/91 _____

g. 12/26/2003 _____

11. **Write a composition choosing either topic A or topic B.** (2 pt. each sentence)

Topic A: Write a note of seven complete Spanish sentences to a pen pal of your age. Describe your daily activities or schedule. Include activities such as getting up, studying, hobbies, etc. State at what times you do these activities.

Topic B: You have just secured a job interview (*una entrevista*) for tomorrow. You write a note of seven complete Spanish sentences to a parent. Explain how you are getting ready for it. What time is it? How will you dress yourself? How will you travel there? Who is interviewing you?

_____

_____

_____

_____

_____

_____

_____

_____

_____

_____

_____

_____

LISTENING EXERCISES V

Exercise 1. Listen for the time in each sentence. Then draw the hands on the analog clock face and write the time on the digital clock face for each statement given. [CD–A, Track 3]

53

Exercise 2. *¿Verdadero o falso?* **Does the date you hear match the one given? The dates are written in the English style. Write** *v* **for** *verdadero* **or** *f* **for** *falso.* **[CD–A, Track 4]**

a. _____ 5/29/86

b. _____ 12/2/90

c. _____ 10/16/91

d. _____ 7/11/95

e. _____ 1/20/99

f. _____ 3/17/84

g. _____ 9/30/98

h. _____ 2/21/92

i. _____ 6/4/94

j. _____ 8/15/81

Exercise 3. **You will hear six different sets of plans. Listen carefully for the date, the time, and the activity. Write down each plan under the appropriate day of the week. Also include the time. Complete sentences are not necessary. You may not have something for each day.**
[CD–A, Track 5]

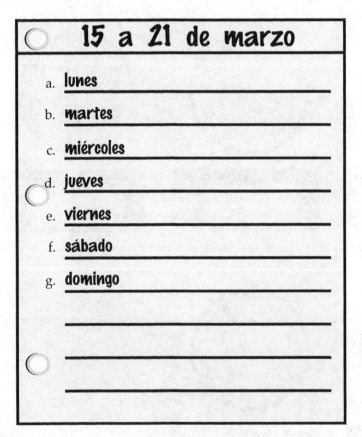

15 a 21 de marzo

a. **lunes** _____

b. **martes** _____

c. **miércoles** _____

d. **jueves** _____

e. **viernes** _____

f. **sábado** _____

g. **domingo** _____

_____

_____

Review the material in this section in preparation for the Self Test. This Self Test will check your mastery of this particular section as well as your knowledge of all previous sections.

SELF TEST 5

5.01   **Write the correct Spanish time given on the digital clock faces.** (1 pt. each)

a. Son las nueve y cinco.

b. Son las siete y media.

c. Es la una.

d. Son las diez menos diez.

e. Son las seis y cuarto.

f. Son las ocho menos cuarto.

g. Es mediodía.

h. Son las cuatro y veinte.

i. Son las doce menos cuarto.

j. Son las dos menos veintinueve.

5.02   **Write the times in Spanish. Spell out all numbers. Include A.M. and P.M.**   (2 pts. each)

a. 8:21 A.M.   _____

b. 6:01 P.M.   _____

c. 12:00 A.M.   _____

d. 11:16 A.M.   _____

e. 10:45 P.M.   _____

f. 1:30 P.M.   _____

g. 9:42 P.M.   _____

h. 4:15 A.M.   _____

i. 2:12 A.M.   _____

j. 5:37 P.M.   _____

5.03 **Fill in the missing words for each date.** (1 pt. each blank)

a. Today is November 30.   Hoy es _____ treinta _____ noviembre.

b. Tomorrow is Saturday, July 5.   _____ es _____ , el cinco de julio.

c. Today is Friday.   _____ es _____ .

d. Yesterday was Thursday, September 30.   Ayer _____ jueves, el _____ de _____ .

e. Today is Monday, August 1.   Hoy _____ lunes, el _____ de agosto.

5.04 **Translate the dates given in the English style. You may leave the years in numerals (for example, 1984).** (2 pts. each)

a. 7/12/98   _____

b. 3/17/92   _____

c. 6/7/67   _____

d. 9/25/90   _____

e. 1/11/11   _____

f. 10/31/81   _____

g. 12/26/76   _____

h. 8/1/84   _____

i. 2/23/70   _____

j. 5/29/98   _____

49 / 61

Score   _____

Adult Check _____

              Initial   Date

VI. REVIEW NOUN/ADJECTIVE AGREEMENT

Benjamín is describing his family for a report for class. **Read his report.**

Mi mamá es muy simpática. Mi papá es simpático también. Ella es baja, pero mi papá no es bajo. Él es alto. Mi mamá es morena, y mi papá es moreno también.

Chela es mi hermana. Ella es divertida y muy responsable. Mis hermanos son jóvenes, y por eso son divertidos, pero no son muy responsables. ¿Y yo? Soy bueno, soy inteligente y soy bajo, como mi mamá. Mi familia es contenta y agradable.

> **List at least two adjectives associated with each person in Benjamín's report.**

6.1   a. Mamá   b. Papá   c. Chela

_____   _____   _____

_____   _____   _____

_____   _____   _____

       d. Los hermanos   e. Benjamín   f. La familia

_____   _____   _____

_____   _____   _____

_____   _____   _____

> **Review the feminine adjectives.**

6.2   In what letter(s) do the adjectives often end? _____

> **Review the masculine adjectives.**

6.3   a. In what letter(s) do they often end? _____

What Benjamín's essay demonstrates is the concept of agreement between nouns and adjectives. As you know, all nouns in Spanish are assigned number and gender.

       b. What is meant by "number"? _____

       c. What is meant by "gender"? _____

You may remember that you will know the number and gender of a noun by looking at its definite or indefinite article. Here are the definite and indefinite articles for your review.

Definite articles		
	masculine	**feminine**
singular	el	la
plural	los	las

6.4   a. What is the gender and number of *la familia*? _____

       b. What is the gender and number of *los hermanos*? _____

Indefinite articles		
	masculine	feminine
singular	un	una
plural	unos	unas

6.5   a.   What is the gender and number of *un dentista*? _____

b.   What is the gender and number of *unas turistas?* _____

As nouns have gender and number, the adjectives must agree with that noun in the same manner. A feminine, singular noun must be followed by a feminine, singular adjective.

Review Benjamín's essay again.

6.6   a.   What words did he use to describe his mother and sister? _____

_____

b.   *Mother* is both feminine and singular. What must be the feminine singular ending for an adjective?

_____

c.   What words described Benjamín and his father? _____

_____

d.   *Father* and *Pepito* are singular nouns. How is a singular masculine adjective ended? _____

_____

e.   By reviewing the adjectives reserved for the brothers, what can you deduce must be the masculine plural ending of adjectives? _____

f.   What would be the feminine plural ending? _____

Summarize the information.

Fill in the chart below with the proper adjective endings.

6.7

	masculine	feminine
singular	a. _____	c. _____
	_____	_____
plural	b. _____	d. _____
	_____	_____

Agreement can be a difficult concept for speakers of English, because this concept does not exist in our language. The hardest part is remembering to make nouns and adjectives agree in number and gender every single time you write or speak Spanish. Some final points to remember:

A.   Most adjectives are placed **after** the nouns they modify. For example,
     la casa amarilla **(the house yellow)**.

Exceptions to this rule are:	buen(a)	(good)
	mal(a)	(bad)
	nuevo(a)	(new)
		adjectives of quantity (mucho, todo, poco, etc.)

Some adjectives may be written before or after their nouns. They must, of course, agree in number and gender. *Bueno* and *malo* drop the *o* before masculine singular nouns.

> la buena chica (the good girl) or la chica buena
> el buen señor (the good man) or el señor bueno
> el mal perro (the bad dog) or el perro malo
> los nuevos autos (the new cars) or los autos nuevos

B.   Did you notice from Benjamín's report that the word *responsable* kept its *e* for Chela and the brothers? Did you notice that *e* is an ending for both masculine and feminine adjectives? Only those adjectives ending in *o, os* or *a, as* have a spelling change to show gender. Adjectives ending in *e* have no spelling change other than to add an *s* to agree in number. Adjectives ending in a consonant (except for those denoting nationality) will simply add *s* for the plural form. There is no distinction of gender.

> el chico agradable / popular
> la chica agradable / popular
> los chicos agradables / populares
> las chicas agradables / populares

C.   Adjectives of nationality that do not end in *o* are also exceptions.

6.8   a.   Using the chart below, list an example adjective of nationality that is an exception. _____

       b.   List an example of an adjective of nationality that is regular. _____

In most cases, feminine endings are placed on these words. To give you an idea of what is being expressed, a few of the forms are listed. Note that the accent mark appears only on some of the masculine singular forms of adjectives of nationality ending in a consonant. This is because the other three forms add an extra syllable, which allows the stress to naturally occur on the same syllable as for the masculine singular form.

Spanish:	español, española, españoles, españolas
French:	francés, francesa, franceses, francesas
English:	inglés, inglesa, ingleses, inglesas
Cuban:	cubano, cubana cubanos, cubanas
Italian:	italiano, italiana, italianos, italianas

SUPPLEMENTAL VOCABULARY

aburrido	bored, boring	irresponsable	irresponsible
agradable	friendly, pleasant	irritado	annoyed, irritated
alto	tall	joven	young
antipático	mean, unpleasant	mal	poorly, badly
bajo	short	malo	bad
bien	well, fine	moreno	brunette
bonito	pretty	nervioso	nervous
bueno	good	paciente	patient
contento	happy	pelirrojo	red-haired
desilusionado	disappointed	pequeño	small
divertido	funny, amusing	popular	popular
enfermo	sick	preocupado	worried
enojado	angry	responsable	responsible
grande	large, big	rubio	blonde
guapo	handsome	simpático	pleasant, nice
impaciente	impatient	triste	sad
inteligente	smart	viejo	old

 Change the adjective in the first sentence to agree with the new subject in the second.

6.9   a.   La chica está aburrida. Las chicas están _____ .

b.   Nosotros somos morenos. Nosotras somos _____ .

c.   Alonso está preocupado. Mis hermanas están _____ .

d.   Tú eres popular. El estudiante es _____ .

e.   Mi madre es simpática. Tus padres son _____ .

f.   La película es buena. El picnic es _____ .

g.   Los libros son viejos. La casa es _____ .

h.   El cerro es grande. Las montañas son _____ .

i.   La manta es amarilla. El mantel es _____ .

j.   La escuela es divertida. Las clases son _____ .

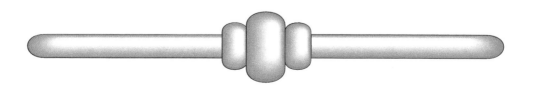

Change each adjective to agree with the new subject.

6.10   1. los señores malos

      a. alto   b. francés   c. simpática   d. inteligente

      a. _____   b. _____   c. _____   d. _____

     2. el chico bueno

      a. agradables   b. inteligente   c. joven   d. morena

      a. _____   b. _____   c. _____   d. _____

     3. unas clases grandes

      a. pequeño   b. español   c. simpático   d. difícil

      a. _____   b. _____   c. _____   d. _____

     4. las amigas fieles

      a. rubio   b. alto   c. simpático   d. alemán

      a. _____   b. _____   c. _____   d. _____

     5. una familia grande

      a. pelirrojo   b. nervioso   c. agradable   d. español

      a. _____   b. _____   c. _____   d. _____

Translate into Spanish. Work from the nouns given and the supplemental vocabulary.

una película	el libro
unas tareas	una señora
un gato	una clase
los perros	el consejo
los hombres	una casa

6.11   a. a red house   _____

      b. a patient lady   _____

      c. an interesting class   _____

      d. the good advice   _____

      e. the new book   _____

      f. some big assignments   _____

      g. the English men   _____

      h. the bad dogs   _____

      i. a sad cat   _____

      j. a popular movie   _____

READING COMPREHENSION

Read the paragraph below and complete the following activities.

Me llamo Carmen. Soy argentina y hago planes para una fiesta de bienvenida para el nuevo estudiante de intercambio que va a vivir con nosotros por un año. Entiendo que es inteligente y simpático. Tiene quince años. Es alto y moreno. (Me olvido de su nombre ahora mismo.) Quiero invitar a una variedad de amigos. Quiero una fiesta interesante. Él va a conocer a muchas personas diferentes. Conozco a algunas personas divertidas. Mi mejor amiga es muy estudiosa. Dos amigos son atléticos. Otros amigos son músicos. El hermano de mi mejor amiga es muy, muy guapo. ¡Cuánto me alegro!

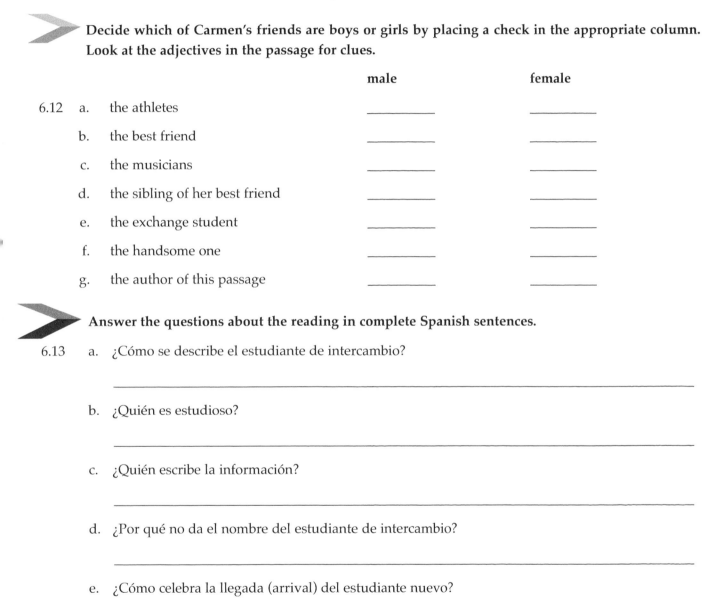

Decide which of Carmen's friends are boys or girls by placing a check in the appropriate column. Look at the adjectives in the passage for clues.

		male	female
6.12	a. the athletes	_____	_____
	b. the best friend	_____	_____
	c. the musicians	_____	_____
	d. the sibling of her best friend	_____	_____
	e. the exchange student	_____	_____
	f. the handsome one	_____	_____
	g. the author of this passage	_____	_____

Answer the questions about the reading in complete Spanish sentences.

6.13 a. ¿Cómo se describe el estudiante de intercambio?

_____

b. ¿Quién es estudioso?

_____

c. ¿Quién escribe la información?

_____

d. ¿Por qué no da el nombre del estudiante de intercambio?

_____

e. ¿Cómo celebra la llegada (arrival) del estudiante nuevo?

_____

✔ Adult check _____
　　　　　　　　　　　　　　Initial　　　　　　　　　　　　　　　　Date

 Review the material in this section in preparation for the Self Test. This Self Test will check your mastery of this particular section as well as your knowledge of all previous sections.

SELF TEST 6

6.01   **Write the opposite.** (1 pt. each)

a.   alto / _____

b.   interesante / _____

c.   moreno / _____

d.   joven / _____

e.   impaciente / _____

f.   antipático / _____

g.   bueno / _____

h.   mal / _____

i.   feo / _____

j.   responsable / _____

6.02   **Change the adjective at the head of each group of nouns to agree in number and gender with those nouns.** (1 pt. each blank)

              a.   **pelirrojo**

la mujer   _____

las personas   _____

los hermanos   _____

              b.   **paciente**

el oculista   _____

la enfermera   _____

las señoras   _____

              c.   **francés**

los bebés   _____

las estudiantes   _____

el artista   _____

              d.   **aburrido**

las clases   _____

el examen   _____

los hombres   _____

              e.   **español**

mi hermana   _____

los tíos   _____

el señor   _____

              f.   **popular**

la profesora   _____

mis hermanas   _____

los perros   _____

6.03   **Express what items you currently have, using the cues given and the correct form of the verb** *tener* **(to have).** (2 pts. each)

a.   ¿Cuál bolsa es de ti? (the blue bag)

_____

b.   ¿Cuál hermana es de ellos? (the blonde sister)

_____

c.   ¿Cuál libro es de Uds.? (the small book)

_____

d. ¿Cuáles chicos son amigos de Ud.? (the smart friends)

_____

e. ¿A cuáles profesores conoces? (some good teachers)

_____

6.04   **Unscramble the phrases in order to make a logical translation. Also make sure all the nouns and adjectives agree.** (2 pts. each)

a. a good game   juego/un/bueno_____

b. a short lady   una/bajo/señora _____

c. the new house   nuevo/casa/la _____

d. the bad dogs   los/perros/malo _____

e. the difficult tests   exámenes/difícil/los _____

f. the French song   francés/la/canción _____

g. the old school   viejo/escuela/la _____

h. a large car   un/grande/coche _____

i. some irritated students estudiantes/irritado/unas _____

j. some bad grades   malo/notas/unas _____

VII. REVIEW *SER* AND *ESTAR*

Before reviewing the rules, let's write the forms for the sake of reference.

 Write the forms of *SER* in the chart below.

7.1   **ser**—to be

a. yo	d. nosotros nosotras
b. tú	e. vosotros vosotras
c. él ella Ud.	f. ellos ellas Uds.

Write the forms of *ESTAR* in the chart below.

7.2   **estar**—to be

a. yo	d. nosotros nosotras
b. tú	e. vosotros vosotras
c. él ella Ud.	f. ellos ellas Uds.

Ser and *estar* both mean *to be*, but they are not used interchangeably. Review the rules by examining these verbs within sentences:

    a.   Yo soy de la Argentina.

    b.   Yo estoy en Nueva York hoy.

There are two kinds of information given.

7.3   1.   Sentence **a** is describing _____ . Which verb is used? _____

2. Sentence **b** is describing _____ . Which verb is used? _____

    c. Ella es simpática. Tiene muchos amigos.

    d. Ella está contenta porque visita con su amigo.

Again, we are reading two kinds of information about this girl.

3. Sentence **c** tells us _____ . Which verb is used? _____

4. Sentence **d** tells us _____ . Which verb is used? _____

    e. Son las seis de la mañana.

    f. Ud. es policía.

    g. Mañana es jueves.

When learning to choose between the two verbs, we always have to ask ourselves what kind of information is communicated in the sentence.

5. Sentence **e** tells us _____ . Which verb is used? _____

6. Sentence **f** tells us _____ . Which verb is used? _____

7. Sentence **g** tells us _____ . Which verb is used? _____

> **Organize these conclusions into a table for easy reference. Fill in the table as you answer the questions.**

7.4   a. Which verb discussed origin?

       b. Which verb discussed location?

       c. Which verb denoted a personality trait?

       d. Which implied (temporary) emotions?

       e. How was profession expressed?

       f. With which verb were date and time expressed?

SER	ESTAR

A few points to remember:

Estar is used for permanent or temporary locations.

Example:	La capital de Colorado está en Denver.
	Mi casa está en la calle Roble.

67

Ser is for personality traits or qualities that are important to the identity of a person or object. Therefore, **color** and **age** are denoted by *ser*.

> **Example:** Yo soy rubio.
>
> Tú eres joven. (Even though "you" will age, being young is important to who you are, so we must use *eres*.)

Being a student counts as a job! Also, it's important to a person's identity.

Remember that the verb you choose for your sentence will determine that phrase's meaning. Read the following sentences.

Ella está aburrida. (She is **bored**.)

Está implies a temporary state—bored.

Ella es aburrida. (She is **boring**.)

Es implies a permanent condition or personality trait—boring.

Here are some adjectives that change meaning when they are used with *ser* or *estar*.

ser listo—to be clever	estar listo—to be ready
ser enfermo—to be sickly (poor health)	estar enfermo—to be ill (from which you would recover)
ser malo—to be a bad person, evil	estar malo—to feel sick
ser nervioso—to be jumpy, nervous	estar nervioso—to be nervous (about something)
ser frío—to be cold (naturally, like an ice cube)	estar frío—to be cold, to have cooled off

 Practice the forms of *ser* by stating where each person is from, using the above map.

7.5

a. Elisa y Juana _____ de _____ .

b. Uds. _____ de _____ .

c. Ud. _____ de _____ .

d. Yo _____ de _____ .

e. Las estudiantes _____ de _____ .

f. Ramón _____ de _____ .

g. Nosotros _____ de _____ .

h. María _____ de _____ .

i. Manuela y Ud. _____ de _____ .

j. Y tú _____ de _____ .

Use the picture below to fill in the blanks for Exercise 7.6.

Practice the forms of *estar*. State where each person is located in the house right now.

7.6   a.   Nosotros _____ en _____ .

      b.   Tú _____ en _____ .

      c.   La abuela _____ en _____ .

      d.   Los padres _____ en _____ .

      e.   Yo _____ en _____ .

      f.   El hermano _____ en _____ .

      g.   Ud. _____ en _____ .

      h.   Paco _____ en _____ .

      i.   Las hermanas _____ en _____ .

      j.   Mi tía _____ en _____ .

> Review using the verbs in sentences. Circle the verb that completes the meaning of each sentence. Use the chart you completed in Exercise 7.4 as a guide.

7.7
a. (Estoy, Soy) de Chile.

b. En clase (estamos, somos) contentos.

c. El color del coche (está, es) azul.

d. Tú (estás, eres) rubio.

e. Uds. (están, son) en el hospital.

f. Mis amigos (están, son) profesores.

g. Los libros no (están, son) nuevos.

h. El anillo (está, es) de plata.

i. (Está, Es) la una.

j. Hoy (estoy, soy) enferma.

k. Hoy (está, es) miércoles.

l. Ella siempre (está, es) deprimida.

m. La señora (está, es) francesa.

n. El plato (está, es) en la mesa.

o. Nosotros (estamos, somos) pobres.

> Fill in the blanks with a form of *ser* or *estar*.

7.8
a. Enrique _____ un chico de catorce años. _____ chileno. Aunque _____ joven, tiene un trabajo. Él _____ periodista. Escribe artículos para el periódico. Su jefe dice que Enrique _____ buen trabajador. Nunca _____ tarde.

b. Mis hermanas _____ mayores que yo. Cada día _____ en sus clases en la universidad. _____ muy inteligentes. Hoy no _____ allí. _____ de vacaciones y _____ en casa conmigo. Me gusta porque ellas _____ divertidas.

c. Cuando nosotros _____ juntos (together), _____ muy contentos. _____ muy buenos amigos. Al mediodía, probablemente _____ en el parque, montando en bicicleta. _____ atléticos. _____ en las mismas clases y nuestras casas _____ en la misma calle.

> Complete the sentences with a form of *ser* or *estar* as needed by the translations.

7.9
a. La chica _____ aburrida. (She is boring.)

   La chica _____ aburrida. (She is bored.)

b. Nosotros _____ listos. (We are clever.)

   Nosotros _____ listos. (We are ready.)

c. _____ cansados. (They are tired.)

   _____ cansados. (They are tiresome.)

d. _____ irritados. (They are irritated.)

   _____ irritados. (They are irritating.)

e. Tú _____ enferma. (You are sickly.)

   Tú _____ enferma. (You are sick.)

> **Translate the following phrases into Spanish. Use the vocabulary list at the end of the chapter.**

7.10   a.   I am not a teacher.   _____

        b.   They are old.   _____

        c.   You are brunette.   _____

        d.   She's in class.   _____

        e.   You are Spanish.   _____

        f.   The movie is boring.   _____

        g.   Today is May 23.   _____

        h.   We're disappointed.   _____

        i.   All of you aren't home.   _____

        j.   The car is red.   _____

READING COMPREHENSION

Read the following passage out loud. Complete the following activities.

Aquí está mi cuarto. Es muy cómodo. Estoy sola en mi dormitorio porque no tengo que compartirlo con mi hermano. Mi dormitorio no es muy grande, pero hay espacio para todo. Mi cama está a la derecha de mi tocador. El armario es pequeño; está a la izquierda del tocador. Y mi escritorio está entre dos ventanas. Hay una lámpara allí. Mi reloj está allí también. Mi cuarto es azul claro, con las cortinas rosadas. También es limpio; yo soy una persona ordenada. No me gusta el lío. Me gusta mucho la música, y por eso en las paredes hay muchos carteles de los músicos populares. Soy artista un poco, y mis dibujos y pinturas están al lado de los carteles. Normalmente, por la noche, estoy en mi cuarto, haciendo la tarea o charlando con amigos por teléfono.

compartir	to share	espacio	space
el tocador	dresser	el reloj	clock
allí	there	azul claro	light blue
arreglado	tidy	el lío	the mess
el cartel	poster	el dibujo	the drawing
haciendo	doing	charlando	chatting

Find the fifteen forms of *ser* **and** *estar* **found in the passage and write them on the lines. State why a form of** *ser* **or** *estar* **has been used (location, personality trait, etc.). Remember to use the chart from Exercise 7.4 as a guide.**

7.11 a. _____   i. _____

      b. _____   j. _____

      c. _____   k. _____

      d. _____   l. _____

      e. _____   m. _____

      f. _____   n. _____

      g. _____   o. _____

      h. _____   p. **bonus: What word is used in place of *estar*? _____**

Answer the following questions about the passage in English.

7.12 a. Does she like her room? How do you know?

        _____

      b. Name something she really enjoys.

        _____

      c. What furniture does she own?

        _____

      d. How many siblings does she have?

        _____

      e. How can we be sure the author is a female?

        _____

Now, answer in Spanish.

7.13 a. ¿De qué colores es el cuarto?

        _____

      b. ¿Hay un lío grande en el cuarto?

        _____

      c. ¿Cómo describe la talla (the size) del cuarto?

        _____

      d. ¿Cuáles objetos están sobre el escritorio?

        _____

      e. Describe dónde están dos muebles en el cuarto.

        _____

 **LISTENING EXERCISES VII**

> **Exercise 1.** Listen for the verb form in each sentence. Decide which form of *estar* to write in the blank, based on the form you hear. [CD–A, Track 6]

a. _____ enferma.

b. La capital _____ en Nueva York.

c. _____ tarde.

d. _____ en la biblioteca.

e. _____ en el consultorio.

> **Exercise 2.** Listen for the verb form in each sentence. Decide which form of *ser* to write in the blank, based on the form you hear. [CD–A, Track 7]

a. _____ enfermeros.

b. _____ atlético.

c. _____ enfermo.

d. _____ felices.

e. _____ inteligente.

> **Exercise 3.** Now decide which verb to use, *ser* or *estar*. Complete the sentences with the correct form of the verb you have chosen. [CD–A, Track 8]

a. _____ en su apartamento.

b. _____ cubanos.

c. _____ las doce.

d. Yo _____ frustrada.

e. Uds. _____ deprimidas.

f. _____ artista.

g. _____ estudiante.

h. Hoy _____ jueves.

i. _____ en el estante.

j. Nosotros _____ bien, gracias.

 Review the material in this section in preparation for the Self Test. This Self Test will check your mastery of this particular section as well as your knowledge of all previous sections.

SELF TEST 7

7.01 **Give three situations when *ser* is used.** (1 pt. each)

a. _____

b. _____

c. _____

7.02 **Give two situations when *estar* is used.** (1 pt. each)

a. _____

b. _____

7.03 **Give the correct form of *ser* or *estar*.** (1 pt. each)

1. Hoy **(a)** _____ miércoles. **(b)** _____ las diez de la mañana. Linda

   (c) _____ aburrida porque dice que todos los días la clase de matemáticas

   (d) _____ muy aburrida. Ella **(e)** _____ contenta al fin de esta clase.

2. La casa de Jorge **(f)** _____ en la Avenida Embarque pero ahora él no

   (g) _____ en casa. Él **(h)** _____ estudiante y **(i)** _____ en la

   biblioteca para cumplir su tarea. **(j)** _____ un muchacho muy inteligente.

3. La tienda más grande en el centro **(k)** _____ cerca del parque. Yo

   (l) _____ enfermera y trabajo en el hospital que **(m)** _____ enfrente de la

   tienda. Mis padres **(n)** _____ doctores y **(o)** _____ españoles. Ahora ellos

   (p) _____ en México.

4. Nosotros **(q)** _____ altos y rubios pero nuestros primos **(r)** _____ bajos y

   morenos. Mi primo Pablo **(s)** _____ enfermo hoy y no **(t)** _____ con la

   familia en la fiesta. Pablo **(u)** _____ muy divertido y también **(v)** _____

   muy listo.

5. Por la mañana siempre llegamos a la escuela a las ocho. Hoy llegamos tarde porque ya

   (w) _____ las ocho y media. El coche no va porque la llanta **(x)** _____

   ponchada (flat) y nosotros no podemos **(y)** _____ en la escuela a tiempo. El profesor

   (z) _____ muy simpático y no **(aa)** _____ enojado.

26
32

Score _____

Adult Check _____

Initial   Date

75

VIII. REVIEW THE PRESENT PROGRESSIVE AND REFLEXIVE VERBS

A
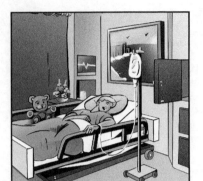

B

C

D

E

INTRODUCTORY READING

 Using the pictures above, write the letter of the picture next to its written description.

8.1   a. _____   Los chicos están jugando al básquetbol. Están haciendo ejercicios. Están practicando.

b. _____   La esposa y su esposo están comprando la comida. Están pagando cincuenta dólares.

c. _____   El estudiante está estudiando. No está durmiendo esta noche.

d. _____   Ella está nadando, aunque ahora está saliendo del agua. Está tomando el sol.

e. _____   El señor no se está sintiendo bien. Está descansando en el hospital.

From what infinitive does each form come?

8.2   a.   están jugando   _____

b.   están comprando   _____

c.   está estudiando   _____

d.   está nadando   _____

e.   se está sintiendo   _____

Complete the following questions.

8.3   a.   If *jugar* is "to play," translate *están jugando*.   _____

b.   If *comprar* is "to buy," translate *están comprando*.   _____

c.   If *estudiar* is "to study," translate *está estudiando*.   _____

d.   If *nadar* is "to swim," translate *está nadando*.   _____

e.   If *cantar* is "to sing," translate *estamos cantando*.   _____

The present progressive is translated as *to be doing…(something)*. It can be used interchangeably with the simple present tense, although it is mostly used to stress the immediacy of an action. Review the formation of the present progressive. It is a compound tense because its forms require two parts, or words.

Fill in the blanks to complete the statements.

8.4   a.   The first half of a _____ form is an agreeing form of the verb _____ .
The form of _____ translates as _____ .

b.   The _____ half of a progressive form is the present participle. For "AR" verbs
the present participle ending is _____ . For "IR" and "ER" verbs, the ending is
_____ .

Look at the reading passages again.

8.5   a.   How do all the present participles end? _____

b.   Does that ending change to agree with the subject? _____

Note: *Estar* changes to agree with the subject. Its job is to establish the subject of the sentence (and its forms mean "am," "is," or "are"). The **present participle** remains the same; that is, it ends in *–ando* or *–iendo* no matter the number or gender of the subject.

Put all this information together by filling in the chart below with the present progressive forms of the verbs *trabajar* (to work), *comer* (to eat), and *vivir* (to live).

8.6   **trabajar**—to work

a. yo	d. nosotros nosotras
b. tú	e. vosotros vosotras
c. él ella Ud.	f. ellos ellas Uds.

Answer the following questions.

8.7　a.　Which form means "I am working"? _____

　　　b.　Translate *estamos trabajando.* _____

8.8　　　**comer**—to eat

a.　yo	d.　nosotros 　　nosotras
b.　tú	e.　vosotros 　　vosotras
c.　él 　　ella 　　Ud.	f.　ellos 　　ellas 　　Uds.

 Answer the following questions.

8.9　a.　Translate *estás comiendo.* _____

　　　b.　Translate *estamos comiendo.* _____

8.10　　**vivir**—to live

a.　yo	d.　nosotros 　　nosotras
b.　tú	e.　vosotros 　　vosotras
c.　él 　　ella 　　Ud.	f.　ellos 　　ellas 　　Uds.

 Answer the following questions.

8.11　a.　Translate *estoy viviendo.* _____

　　　b.　Translate *él está viviendo.* _____

Memorize the spelling-change and irregular present participles listed below.

I. Infinitives ending in **–aer, –uir, –eer**

    a. The letter *i* of *-iendo* is replaced with *y* for the sake of pronunciation.

        1. *caer* (to fall)—*cayendo* (falling)

        2. *construir* (to build)—*construyendo* (building)

        3. *creer* (to believe)—*creyendo* (believing)

        4. *leer* (to read*)—leyendo* (reading)

        5. *traer* (to bring)—*trayendo* (bringing)

    b. The verbs *oír* (to hear) and *ir* (to go) are also included in this group—*oyendo* (hearing) and *yendo* (going)

II. Infinitives known as "IR" shoe verbs

    a. For the present participle of some verbs, the spelling change is *e–i*.

        1. *preferir* (to prefer)—*prefiriendo* (preferring)

        2. *divertirse* (to have fun)—*divirtiéndose* (having fun)

    b. This is also the case for the following infinitives.

        1. *decir* (to say, tell)—*diciendo* (saying, telling)

        2. *venir* (to come)—*viniendo* (coming)

    c. For the present participle of other verbs, the spelling change is *o–u*.

        1. *dormir* (to sleep)—*durmiendo* (sleeping)

        2. *morir* (to die)—*muriendo* (dying)

Finally…

The present participle can also be used with the following verbs to suggest an ongoing action.

    seguir (to follow, continue)

    continuar (to keep on, continue)

      Sigo estudiando. I continue studying.

      Continuamos trabajando. We keep on working.

Pronouns are to be placed in front of or after the entire form; the two words that make up the form must never be split.

    Me estoy lavando (Estoy lavándome). I am washing up.

    ¿No la está encontrando? (¿No está encontrándola?) Aren't you meeting her?

 Write the present progressive forms of the given infinitives.

8.12 a. caminar (tú) _____

     b. leer (Mario) _____

     c. salir (las clases) _____

     d. jugar (Juana y yo) _____

     e. decir (yo) _____

     f. vivir (Uds.) _____

     g. buscar (tú) _____

     h. traer (ellos y yo) _____

     i. oír (yo) _____

     j. beber (mi mamá) _____

Change the simple present tense forms to the present progressive.

8.13 a.   ellas se encuentran _____

       b.   no escribo _____

       c.   ¿no jugamos? _____

       d.   quiere _____

       e.   estudio _____

       f.   sube _____

       g.   ¿oyes tú? _____

       h.   se muere _____

       i.   no comen _____

Use the list of infinitives below to translate the phrases into Spanish. All are used once.

cantar	escribir	dormir	oír
venir	cerrar	pedir	poner

8.14 a.   She is hearing voices *(voces)*. _____

       b.   We are closing the door. _____

       c.   I am not setting the table now. _____

       d.   Alonzo and Diego are sleeping. _____

       e.   Juan and I are coming. _____

       f.   You (Ud.) are singing. _____

       g.   All of you (Uds.) are writing letters. _____

       h.   We are asking for money. _____

Answer, using a present progressive form in your response.

8.15 a.   ¿Qué estás haciendo ahora? _____

       b.   ¿Qué está haciendo tu papá ahora? _____

       c.   ¿Está hablando la profesora ahora? _____

       d.   ¿Qué estás esperando en el futuro? _____

       e.   ¿Con quién estás almorzando esta tarde? _____

✔ Adult check _____
                                        Initial   Date

Exercise 1. Listen to each present progressive phrase. On your activity sheet, circle the subject of each sentence you hear. [CD–A, Track 9]

1. a. yo   b. tú   c. ellos

2. a. yo   b. tú y yo   c. tú

3. a. tú   b. mi amigo   c. nosotros

4. a. Uds.   b. ellos   c. nosotros

Exercise 2. Change the (simple) present tense form you hear to the corresponding form of the present progressive. [CD–A, Track 10]

a. Pero ahora _____ café.

b. Pero ahora _____ el jazz ahora.

c. Pero hoy _____ con un lápiz.

d. Pero esta semana _____ al supermercado el sábado.

e. Pero hoy _____ las películas.

f. Pero ahora no _____ en el parque.

g. Pero hoy no _____ la lección.

h. Pero ahora, _____ en esta práctica.

i. Pero hoy no _____ papel a la clase.

j. Pero hoy _____ al mediodía.

a. _____

b. _____

c. _____

d. _____

e. _____

f. _____

g. _____

h. _____

i. _____

j. _____

READING COMPREHENSION

Read the story below.

El Sr. Gómez duerme muy bien hasta las ocho y cuarto. En ese momento (quién sabe por qué) se despierta. Se levanta muy de prisa y corre al baño. Se ducha tan rápido que casi no se moja. Se afeita sin prestarse mucha atención y se corta la cara en tres lugares. No hay ni siquiera un minuto para desayunarse. El Sr. Gómez se va sin besar a su esposa ni despedirse de ella. Se mira en el espejo del coche. ¡Se olvidó de peinarse el pelo! Se pone el sombrero para cubrir la cabeza. Se va muy de prisa a la oficina, donde se sienta al escritorio, totalmente rendido. Se duerme otra vez…

 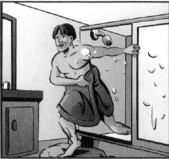  

The passage you just read contained quite a few reflexive verb forms and infinitives. As you remember, the reflexive connotes that the subject is performing an action on him/herself. Like a mirror that reflects an image, the action of a reflexive sentence "bounces back" to the subject.

Write an example of an English reflexive sentence.

8.16   a.   _____

Explain why this phrase is a non-reflexive statement.

I cut the grass.

b.   _____

✔ Adult check _____

                              Initial   Date

Read the sentences below and decide which are reflexive and which are non-reflexive. Make your choice as "reflexive" and "non" in the blanks provided.

8.17   a.   Nos quitamos los abrigos.   _____

        b.   Él lava el coche.   _____

        c.   Mi mamá pone los platos en la mesa.   _____

        d.   Me visto del traje verde.   _____

        e.   Tú bañas a tu hermano menor.   _____

Review the forms by scanning the original reading assignment. Almost all of the verb forms are accompanied by the pronoun *se*. Since it is part of a reflexive expression, what kind of pronoun must it be? A reflexive expression must contain two elements: a verb form and an agreeing reflexive pronoun. Here are the forms of *bañarse*. Pay attention to all elements of the forms.

bañarse—to bathe oneself

yo	**me baño**	nosotros nosotras	**nos bañamos**
tú	**te bañas**	vosotros vosotras	**os bañáis**
él ella Ud.	**se baña**	ellos ellas Uds.	**se bañan**

As you can see, *bañarse* is a regular "AR" verb with the reflexive pronoun placed in front of its verb forms. *Bañarse* is translated as "to bathe oneself." Often the subject pronoun is omitted from the reflexive form in everyday speech. Between the form ending and the reflexive pronoun, it's clear who the subject is.

Translate the forms below.

If *bañarse* means *to bathe oneself*, and *yo* means *I*:

8.18   a.   how do you translate "(yo) me baño"? _____

      b.   (Tú) te bañas.   _____

      c.   (Él) se baña.   _____

      d.   (Ella) se baña.   _____

      e.   (Ud.) se baña.   _____

      f.   (Nosotros/Nosotras) nos bañamos. _____

      g.   (Ellos/Ellas) se bañan.   _____

      h.   (Uds.) se bañan.   _____

Try conjugating the reflexive infinitive *ponerse* (to put on [oneself]).

8.19   Remember, your forms will have two words: the pronoun (first) and a form of *poner*.

ponerse—to put on oneself

a. yo	d. nosotros nosotras
b. tú	e. vosotros vosotras
c. él ella Ud.	f. ellos ellas Uds.

Complete the following questions.

8.20   a.   Translate "they put on (themselves)." _____

b.   Translate "we put on (ourselves)." _____

c.   Which form means "I put on (myself)?" _____

SOME FINAL NOTES

A.   *No* is placed in front of the reflexive pronoun.

No me voy a las siete. (I don't leave at seven o'clock.)

B.   The reflexive pronouns may be placed at the end as well as the beginning of an infinitive construction.

No quiero ponerme la chaqueta.

No me quiero poner la chaqueta. (I don't want to put on my jacket.)

C.   With certain expressions, the reflexive pronoun translates as *each other*.

Los amigos se abrazan. (The friends hug each other.)

Nos hablamos. (We're talking to each other.)

SUPPLEMENTAL VOCABULARY

abrazarse	to hug, embrace each other	irse	to leave, go away
acostarse	to go to bed	lavarse	to wash oneself
afeitarse	to shave oneself	levantarse	to get up
amarse	to love each other	llamarse	to be named (call oneself)
bañarse	to bathe oneself	maquillarse	to put makeup on oneself
besarse	to kiss each other	mirarse	to look at oneself
cepillarse	to brush (one's hair or teeth)	morirse	to die
cortarse	to cut oneself	peinarse	to comb (one's hair)
darse prisa	to be in a hurry	ponerse	to put on oneself
despertarse	to awaken, wake up	quitarse	to take off oneself
divertirse	to enjoy oneself, have fun	sentirse	to feel (emotion)
dormirse	to fall asleep	vestirse	to get dressed

Write the *yo* and *nosotros* forms of each reflexive infinitive. Make sure your answers have both parts: the agreeing pronoun and the verb form.

yo   nosotros

8.21 a. bañarse _____ _____

b. vestirse _____ _____

c. sentirse _____ _____

d. mirarse _____ _____

e. ponerse _____ _____

f. quitarse _____ _____

g. dormirse _____ _____

h. irse _____ _____

i. lavarse _____ _____

j. afeitarse _____ _____

Fill in the missing reflexive pronoun or verb.

8.22 a. _____ lavamos   f. _____ duermo

b. te _____ (quitar)   g. _____ bajas del peso

c. se _____ (divertir)   h. _____ arreglan

d. me _____ (mirar)   i. _____ maquillamos

e. _____ van   j. _____ afeitan

For each group, order the actions in logical sequence (bathing would be listed before getting dressed, for example). As you write the newly ordered list, change the infinitives to the given form. Follow the example.

Example: vestirse / irse / bañarse (tú)
te bañas / te vistes / te vas

8.23 a. quitarse la ropa / dormirse / ponerse los pijamas (él)

_____

b. ducharse / vestirse / despertarse (nosotros)

_____

c. divertirse / irse / vestirse (yo)

_____

d. bañarse / levantarse / despertarse (tú)

_____

e. maquillarse / lavarse la cara / cepillarse los dientes (Uds.)

_____

Decide which reflexive infinitive describes the use of each item pictured. Write the given form of that infinitive in the blanks.

8.24

a. _____   b. _____   c. _____   d. _____   e. _____

f. _____   g. _____   h. _____   i. _____   j. _____

Although you may be involved in certain activities, that doesn't mean others are going to do the same thing. Express this using the correct form of *ir + a + infinitive* and the reflexive infinitive. Make sure your pronouns agree with the given subject.

8.25 a.   Yo me peino pero Lupe no _____ .

b.   Yo me baño por la mañana, pero mis hermanitos _____ por la noche.

c.   Me miro en el espejo pero tú no _____ .

d.   Me despierto temprano pero Uds. no _____ hasta las diez.

e.   Me afeito pero por cierto que Elena no _____ .

f.   Te acuestas a las ocho pero nosotros _____ a las diez.

g.   Te duermes bien pero yo no _____ bien.

h.   Te diviertes en la reunión pero Quique y yo no _____ .

i.   Te cortas el pelo pero tus amigas no _____ el pelo nunca.

j.   Te sientes contento pero yo no _____ contenta al recibir las notas.

Practice your writing skills. Describe the pictures, using reflexive vocabulary as the main actions. Write three sentences for each picture.

8.26

a. El payaso _____

_____

b. Yo _____

_____

c. Paco _____

_____

d. Ellos _____

_____

e. Nosotros _____

_____

Complete the crossword puzzle.

8.27

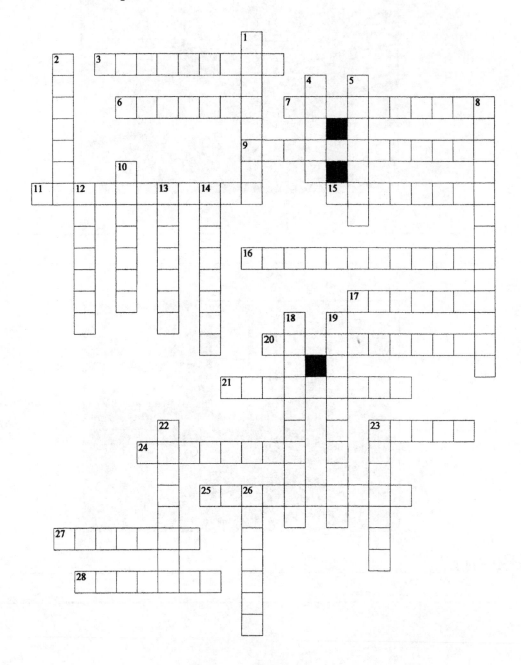

ACROSS

3. they fall asleep
6. you (formal) get dressed
7. they get up
9. we go to bed
11. we get dressed
15. she falls asleep
16. they wake up
17. he showers

20. I wake up
21. I go to bed
23. I leave
24. you (friendly) shower
25. we wash
27. I take off (clothes)
28. I get dressed

DOWN

1. you (friendly) comb
2. I take a shower
4. you (friendly) leave, go
5. they put on (clothes)
8. we get up
10. I comb
12. they wash
13. you (friendly) take a bath

14. I fall asleep
18. you (friendly) go to bed
19. you (friendly) brush
22. you (friendly) take off (clothes)
23. I put on (clothes)
26. they take a bath

> **Exercise 1.** Listen to the following sentences regarding activities that require the reflexive. Write the number of the sentence that matches the pictures below. [CD–A, Track 12]

a. _____

b. _____

c. _____

d. _____

e. _____

f. _____

g. _____

h. _____

i. _____

j. _____

Exercise 2. You and your friends agree with everything your friend Jorge says. Change the reflexive verb form you hear to the *nosotros* form. [CD–A, Track 13]

a. Sí, _____ también.

b. Sí, _____ a la universidad también.

c. Sí, nos gusta _____ tarde también.

d. Sí, _____ a las siete también.

e. Sí, _____ la chaqueta también.

Exercise 3. Agree with your parents' assertions by changing the infinitive you hear to the *yo* form. [CD–A, Track 14]

a. Yo _____ temprano.

b. _____ todos los días.

c. _____ a tiempo a la iglesia.

d. Yo voy a _____ cuando suena el despertador.

e. _____ buena ropa.

Exercise 4. Decide who is the subject in each sentence by listening for the reflexive verb form. Mark an "x" next to your decision. [CD–A, Track 15]

a. Ud. _____ Uds. _____

b. Él _____ Ellos _____

c. Él _____ Ellos _____

d. Ella _____ Ellas _____

e. Ud. _____ Uds. _____

f. Él _____ Ellos _____

g. Ella _____ Nosotros _____

h. Ella _____ Ellas _____

i. Tú _____ Uds. _____

j. Él _____ Ellos _____

Before you take this last Self Test, you may want to do one or more of these self checks.

1. _____ Read the objectives. Determine if you can do them.

2. _____ Restudy the material related to any objectives that you cannot do.

3. _____ Use the SQ3R study procedure to review the material:
   a. Scan the sections.
   b. Question yourself again (review the questions you wrote initially).
   c. Read to answer your questions.
   d. Recite the answers to yourself.
   e. Review areas you didn't understand.

4. _____ Review all activities and Self Tests, writing a correct answer for each wrong answer.

SELF TEST 8

8.01 **Add the correct present participle ending to complete the present progressive forms.** (1 pt. each)

a. (cubrir)   están cubr_____

b. (andar)   estamos and_____

c. (estudiar)   estoy estudi_____

d. (comprender)   estás comprend_____

e. (escribir)   está escrib_____

f. (perder)   estamos perd_____

g. (trabajar)   estoy trabaj_____

h. (vivir)   está viv_____

i. (pensar)   están pens_____

j. (beber)   estás beb_____

8.02 **Fill in the blanks with the correct reflexive pronouns.** (1 pt. each)

a. _____ visto   d. _____ vestimos

b. _____ vistes   e. _____ vestís (extra credit!)

c. _____ viste   f. _____ visten

8.03 **Now decide which pronoun belongs in the proper blank.** (1 pt. each)

a. _____ pongo la chaqueta.   d. ¿_____ estás lavando las manos?

b. Vas a arreglar_____ .   e. Los niños _____ duermen a las siete.

c. No _____ quiere poner ese vestido.

8.04 **Write the correct form of the present progressive twice, each with a correctly (but differently) placed pronoun.** (1 pt. each blank)

a. ponerse (él)   _____   _____

b. afeitarse (Uds.)   _____   _____

c. dormirse (yo)   _____   _____

d. sentirse (los estudiantes)   _____   _____

e. mirarse (Ud.)   _____   _____

f. divertirse (tú)   _____   _____

8.05 **Using the pictures and written cues, state what each person is doing now (a.) in preparation for other activities, and (b) the present progressive to describe the activities. Follow the examples.** (2 pts. each)

sentirse
No se siente bien.

visitar
Está visitando al médico.

1.   a.   acostarse (yo)

_____

_____

b.   hacer un examen

_____

_____

2.   a.   (Concha) bañarse

_____

_____

b.   salir con su novio

_____

_____

3.   a.   levantarse… (nosotros)

_____

_____

b.   viajar a…

_____

_____

4.   a.   vestirse (Juan)

_____

_____

b.   hablar con el supervisor.

_____

_____

8.06   **Change the simple present tense form to the present progressive.** (2 pts. each)

     a.   estudian   _____

     b.   ve   _____

     c.   leo   _____

     d.   traigo   _____

     e.   damos   _____

     f.   te acuestas   _____

     g.   nos vestimos   _____

     h.   dices   _____

     i.   pide   _____

     j.   vuelven   _____

Score   _____

Adult Check   _____

                   Initial   Date

IX. MASTERY EXERCISES

Answer questions about yourself, using complete Spanish sentences.

9.1   a. ¿A qué hora te bañas? _____

        b. ¿A qué hora almuerzas? _____

        c. ¿A qué hora te acuestas? _____

        d. ¿A qué hora vas a la escuela? _____

        e. ¿A qué hora te vistes? _____

Answer questions about your family, using complete Spanish sentences.

        f. ¿ Cuándo se afeita tu padre? _____

        g. ¿Cuándo se desayuna tu madre? _____

        h. ¿Cuándo se duermen tus hermanos(as)? _____

        i. ¿Cuándo se despide de ti tu padre? _____

        j. ¿Cuándo se despierta tu hermano(a)? _____

Describe the images, using a form of *ser* and the adjectives listed below. Make sure everything agrees!

a.    b.

9.2   a. Los globos _____
        b. Mariana y su amiga _____

c.    d.

        c. El joven _____
        d. La enfermera _____

 e.

 f.

e. Tú _____

f. El perro _____

 g.

 h.

g. Nosotros _____

h. Los postres _____

 i.

 j.

i. El agua _____

j. Uds. _____

Matching. The dates are given in English style.

9.3 a. _____ Thurs., 5/15

b. _____ Sat., 7/20

c. _____ Wed., 8/12

d. _____ Sun., 11/13

e. _____ Mon., 12/8

f. _____ Tues., 6/2

g. _____ Fri., 2/27

h. _____ Sat., 1/1

i. _____ Tues., 10/9

1. lunes, el ocho de diciembre

2. sábado, el veinte de julio

3. miércoles, el doce de agosto

4. domingo, el treinta de septiembre

5. viernes, el veintisiete de febrero

6. martes, el nueve de octubre

7. jueves, el quince de mayo

8. sábado, el primero de enero

9. domingo, el trece de noviembre

10. martes, el dos de junio

Use the correct form of the given verb in the following paragraph. Practice the forms of stem-changing (shoe) verbs. Change the bolded verb to agree with each new subject.

9.4 a. En la reunión de mi familia yo **sirvo** el café a los adultos, y mi hermana _____ la leche a los niños. Mis padres _____ bebidas a los otros adultos. Todos nosotros _____ a los parientes para ayudar. (servir)

   b. A la familia González le encantan los deportes. El padre **juega** al golf con su esposa. Ellos _____ el sábado. Su niña, Linda _____ al vólibol en el gimnasio. Todos quieren _____ al fútbol el domingo en el parque. (jugar)

   c. En clase, los estudiantes tratan de **entender** lo más posible. Yo _____ las ciencias fácilmente y mi amigo _____ las matemáticas. Carlos y Elisa, mis otros amigos, _____ todo, parece. Son muy buenos estudiantes. (entender)

   d. Muchas familias mantienen ciertas reglas para conservar órden. En mi familia tenemos que **volver** a casa a unas horas precisas. Yo _____ de la escuela a las cuatro. Mi hermano mayor _____ a las seis para la cena, pero los sábados, nosotros _____ a las siete. (volver)

   e. **Prefiero** comer ensalada para el almuerzo. ¿Y tú? ¿Qué _____ tú comer? Cuando estás con la familia, ¿qué _____ ellos? Mis padres y yo _____ una comida ligera. (preferir)

Translate the following phrases into Spanish.

9.5 a. I speak _____   f. you pass_____

   b. they write _____   g. she understands _____

   c. we study _____   h. they ask for _____

   d. you eat _____   i. I win_____

   e. we go up _____   j. all of you live _____

Fill in the correct form of *ser* or *estar*.

9.6 a. Mi amiga Clarita _____ rubia.

   b. La capital de Colorado _____ Denver.

   c. Denver _____ en Colorado.

   d. Salió mal en el examen. Ahora _____ deprimido.

   e. _____ Diego Macarena.

   f. La fecha _____ el siete de enero.

   g. _____ las dos menos cuarto.

   h. Cinco y tres _____ ocho.

   i. Su casa _____ en el Camino Real.

   j. Tengo gripe. _____ enferma.

Translate into English.

9.7 a. El Sr. Cabra se afeita en el baño a las cinco de la mañana.

_____

_____

b. Preferimos ir al gimnasio juntos.

_____

_____

c. Cuando entro en la escuela, me quito la chaqueta.

_____

_____

d. Ud. se lava la cara antes de que acostarse.

_____

_____

e. Beto y Selena van a la fiesta y se divierten mucho.

_____

_____

Translate into Spanish.

f. I cut myself often when I shave.

_____

_____

g. His grandparents wake up a 6:00 A.M. generally, but today they don't get up until (*hasta*) 7:30.

_____

_____

h. All of you hug and kiss each other at the station.

_____

_____

i. We get dressed and (we) go out.

_____

_____

j. The little girl takes a bath and then falls asleep.

_____

_____

Give the time in Spanish, spelling the numbers in Spanish.

9.8

8:00

a. _____

1:00 A.M.

b. _____

10:06

c. _____

6:30 P.M.

d. _____

9:15

e. _____

2:36

f. _____

2:51 P.M.

g. _____

4:45

h. _____

7:11

i. _____

4:29

j. _____

Circle the verb forms that best complete the meaning of the passage.

9.9

Es viernes. Joselito (**mirando / mirar / mira**) a su hermana mayor, que (**se / te / le**) está preparando para una cita con el novio de ella. Él ve cómo ella se prepara: se (**maquillar / maquilla / maquillo**) y se peina con mucho cuidado.

Cuando Joselito está aburrido de mirarla, anda a la sala. ¡Allí (**es / estando / está**) Papá¡ Papá (**vuelve / va / volver**) del trabajo a las cinco y media en punto todos los días (excepto los sábados y los domingos, claro). (**Son / Tienen / Están**) muy contentos al verse y se abrazan. El chico le (**escribe / muestra / habla**) el examen de historia.

« ¡Ciento por ciento! », (**duerme / despierta / dice**) Papá.

« ¡Qué orgulloso estoy! » Joselito corre a la cocina para decir a mamá que Papá llega.

« Joselito, ayúdame a (**poner / quitar / pone**) la mesa. »

« Bueno, mamí. Yo la (**pongo / pone / quito**) », dice Joselito. Entonces es la hora de comer. Se (**desayunan / almuerzan / cenan**) muy bien.

Después de la cena, la hermana de Joselito (**sale / salir / saliendo**) para su cita. Joselito (**oye / es / hace**) la tarea y (**maquilla / mira / miran**) una película con sus padres.

« (**Es / Son / A**) las nueve », Papá dice. « Joselito, (**es / son / a**) las nueve. Necesitas acostarte. »

« (**Me voy / Me levanto / Irme**) », responde. Y se (**lavando / viste / lava**) la cara y las manos. (**Se peina / Se quita / Se cepilla**) los dientes también. Él y sus padres (**se / nos / te**) besan y se dicen, « Hasta mañana ». El jovencito (**se despierta / se duerme / se acuesta**) y se (**durmiendo / duerme / dan**) de pronto porque (**es / están / está**) en su cama. Joselito (**está / es / ser**) muy bendito en su vida.

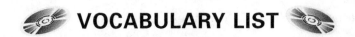

VOCABULARY LIST

abrazarse	to hug, embrace each other	escoger	to choose
abrir	to open	escribir	to write
acostarse (o-ue)	to go to bed	escuchar	to listen to
afeitarse	to shave oneself	escupir	to spit
almorzar (o-ue)	to eat lunch	estar	to be
amarse	to love each other	estudiar	to study
andar	to walk	fregar (e-ie)	to scrub
aprender	to learn	ganar	to win
bailar	to dance	golpear	to hit
bañarse	to bathe oneself	hacer	to do, make
beber	to drink	helar (e-ie)	to freeze
besar	to kiss	hervir (e-ie)	to boil
besarse	to kiss each other	impedir (e-i)	to stop, prevent
buscar	to look (for)	ir	to go
caminar	to walk	irse	to leave, go away
cepillarse	to brush (one's hair or teeth)	jugar (u-ue)	to play (sports)
chiflar	to boo, hiss, whistle	lavarse	to wash oneself
colgar (o-ue)	to hang (up)	leer	to read
comer	to eat	levantarse	to get up
comprender	to understand	llamarse	to be named (call oneself)
conducir	to drive	llevar	to carry, wear, take
confesar (e-ie)	to confess	maquillarse	to put makeup on oneself
conocer	to know (people)	mirar	to look at, watch
conseguir (e-i)	to get, obtain	mirarse	to look at oneself
cortarse	to cut oneself	morir (o-ue)	to die
costar (o-ue)	to cost	morirse (o-ue)	to die
cubrir	to cover	mostrar (o-ue)	to show
dar	to give	negar (e-ie)	to deny
darse prisa	to be in a hurry	ofrecer	to offer
decir	to say, tell	oír	to hear
defender (e-ie)	to defend	pasar	to pass
desayunarse	to eat breakfast	pedir (e-i)	to ask for, order (food)
descansar	to rest	peinarse	to comb (one's hair)
describir	to describe	pensar (e-ie)	to think (about)
despedirse (e-i)	to say good-bye	perder (e-ie)	to lose
despertarse (e-ie)	to awaken, wake up	perseguir (e-i)	to pursue
divertirse (e-ie)	to enjoy oneself, have fun	planear	to plan
dormir (o-ue)	to sleep	poder (o-ue)	to be able, can
dormirse (o-ue)	to fall asleep	poner	to put, place, set
encender (e-ie)	to light, turn on	ponerse	to put on oneself
encontrar (o-ue)	to find, meet	preferir (e-ie)	to prefer
entender (e-ie)	to understand	preparar	to prepare

querer (e-ie)	to want	torcer (o-ue)	to twist
quitarse	to take off oneself	trabajar	to work
regresar	to return	traer	to bring
repetir (e-i)	to repeat	usar	to use
resolver (o-ue)	to solve	vender	to sell
saber	to know (facts, a skill)	venir	to come
salir	to leave, go out	ver	to see
seguir (e-i)	to follow	vestirse (e-i)	to get dressed
sentir (e-ie)	to feel, be sorry	visitar	to visit
sentirse (e-ie)	to feel (emotion)	vivir	to live
ser	to be	volar (o-ue)	to fly
subir	to go up, get on, board	volver (o-ue)	to return
sudar	to sweat	yacer	to lie down
tener	to have		

TIME AND DATE EXPRESSIONS [CD–A, Track 17]

¿A qué hora?	At what time?	lunes	Monday
¿Qué hora es?	What time is it?	martes	Tuesday
¿Cuándo?	When?	miércoles	Wednesday
a eso de…	at about…	jueves	Thursday
a tiempo	on time	viernes	Friday
temprano	early	sábado	Saturday
tarde	late	domingo	Sunday
ahora	now	enero	January
de la mañana	A.M. (in the morning)	febrero	February
de la tarde	P.M. (in the afternoon)	marzo	March
de la noche	P.M. (in the evening)	abril	April
el año	the year	mayo	May
el mes	the month	junio	June
el primero	the first	julio	July
la semana	the week	agosto	August
el día	the day	septiembre	September
el minuto	the minute	octubre	October
la fecha	the date	noviembre	November
la hora	the hour, the time	diciembre	December
hoy es	today is		
mañana es	tomorrow is		
ayer fue	yesterday was		
en punto	on the dot, exactly		
a las/la…	at … o'clock		
medianoche	midnight		
mediodía	noon		

ADJECTIVES AND ADVERBS [CD–A, Track 18]

aburrido	bored, boring	irresponsable	iresponsible
agradable	friendly, pleasant	irritado	annoyed, irritated
alto	tall	joven	young
amable	friendly	listo	clever, ready
antipático	mean, unpleasant	mal	poorly, badly
bajo	short	mal(o)	bad, evil, sick,
bien	well, fine	moreno	brunette
bonito	pretty	nervioso	jumpy, nervous
buen(o)	good	nuevo	new
contento	happy	paciente	patient
deprimido	depressed, sad	pelirrojo	red-haired
desilusionado	disappointed	pequeño	small
divertido	funny, amusing	perfecto	perfect
encantado	delighted	popular	popular
enfermo	sick, sickly	preocupado	worried
enojado	angry	responsable	responsible
frío	cold	rubio	blonde
grande	large, big	simpático	pleasant, nice
guapo	handsome	triste	sad
impaciente	impatient	viejo	old
inteligente	smart		

Before taking the LIFEPAC Test, you may want to do one or more of these self checks.

1. _____ Read the objectives. Check to see if you can do them.

2. _____ Restudy the material related to any objectives that you cannot do.

3. _____ Use the SQ3R study procedure to review the material.

4. _____ Review activities, Self Tests, and LIFEPAC vocabulary words.

5. _____ Restudy areas of weakness indicated by the last Self Test.